Knight Time

Douglas B. Whitley, Jr

DEDICATION

For Douglas and Charles Monroe
I love you.

CONTENTS

Acknowledgments i

1 Betrayal 3

2 Servant of All Pg. 21

3 Spirit of Fear Pg. 81

4 Follow the King Pg. 124

5 The Dagger Pg. 177

ACKNOWLEDGMENTS

Thanks to Mike Avant and the guys of Knights of Adventure who started this journey.

1

BETRAYAL

Jude stood looking out from the tower over the fields surrounding the keep and the woodlands beyond. Bitterness flooded his heart. All this would never be his. He was the younger brother. Gawain would have this. Gawain, the older brother, the favored one, would be Lord of the Manor.

Not that there would be much manor left when the Normans were through.

They had taxed or seized much of the holdings in the country, sometimes fairly, most times not. Even now he knew Flaubert was plotting to gain his father's vast estates. Flaubert's men had approached him, wanting his help. Asking about his father, Sir Barth, about how many men his father had at his command. How many archers? How many swordsmen? He had put them off. To answer them would have been a betrayal. He knew what they wanted. Just then a cock pheasant rose in the millet field to the west.

He watched it rise; wings beating, the long tail feathers streaming out behind it. With incredible speed the falcon fell like a thunder bolt, pinning the cock to the ground. His brother broke from the woods in a trot.

Jude knew he was smiling. Pheasant for the great table. Gawain was always smiling, why should he not. He was the first son. He was a cunning hunter, a fine swordsman, good at learning, well featured. He was even a good brother. Gawain's words echoed in his ears even now. "You will always have a place here. You will always be welcome. You will always have my protection.

As soon as the great farm comes open you shall have that for your very own. Even though I will be Lord of the Manor, I shall not lord it over you, Jude."

They had been just boys then, eleven and twelve, but Gawain had not changed in the last years. Older, yes, a little more serious, but he would say still from time to time, "You will always have a place here. You will always have my protection." Never forgetting the words spoken in youth.

Jude made his way down from the tower into the courtyard to welcome his brother from the hunting. They went in to the great hall. Gawain handing his kills from the hunt, a brace of rabbits, two marsh hens, several pheasants, to the waiting servant.

The two brothers went about their tasks before the evening meal. The days passed, each one rushing into another until now it was early Autumn.

In the village, Jude was at the tanner's seeing to some doe skins his father was having made into soft jerkins and gloves for him and Gawain. There was to be another pair of gloves and a purse for his mother.

Jude was stepping into the street when one of Flaubert's men, Reynard came up to him. "Little brother, you are well met, how is the little one today?" His soft nasals betraying his origins. "My Master was just speaking of you, Mon ami, wondering whether you had thought any more about his . . . . offer, his proposal?" Jude shook off Reynard's arm and drew away. "I have not. Such a thing is not to be countenanced. I will not betray my father's trust." Reynard turned away, but not before Gawain, coming from the fletcher's with an arm full of arrows, saw the two of them together. He rushed to his brother's side. "Stay away from my family, Reynard, fox by name, fox by nature, Norman." As quick as thinking, Reynard drew his dagger even as Gawain dropped the arrows and drew his sword, its point at the Norman's throat "My what quick reflexes you have, big brother, but perhaps the next time you will not be so fortunate, or the place so public. Think on what I have said, little one." With that the Norman backed slowly away from Gawain's sword turned and strode down the lane. "How could you have words with him, Jude?" Gawain rebuked. "I did not have words with him.

I was coming out of the tanners and he spoke to me." said Jude. "What did he want?" Gawain asked. "Only to ask how our father was and if I thought the tanner did good enough work for him to bring a boar hide to him for tanning." Lied Jude. "What would you have to consider about that?" "Do you think I'm lying? He is Norman. How do I know what he's thinking? Gawain had embarrassed him. Treating him like some child. Perhaps he would speak to Flaubert, just to see exactly what he wanted. Perhaps he would do what he wanted to do, not just be the younger brother, the little one.

They made their way home Gawain muttering about the encounter until they reached the great hall. But the episode rankled in Jude's mind. He felt belittled, humiliated.

The more he roiled it over in his mind the more bitter he became. He would see Flaubert. He would make his own decisions.

Some days later Gawain was out trying to catch trout on the rise in the distant stream that flowed through their property. Jude was alone. Silently he slipped from the house and out to the stable. He saddled his horse and followed the path to the village.

Reynard was at the inn with others from Flaubert's following. Jude came in, squinting in the darkness of the room. Reynard saw him and made room for him at the table. "Have a drink," Reynard pushed a flagon toward him spilling some of the mead as he poured. "What brings you here, little one?" Jude spoke into his flagon. "I just happened to be in the village. I came in for a drink. Why did Flaubert want to see me?" With a smile curling about his lips Reynard whispered, "Come and see. We will ride up to the castle and Flaubert can tell you himself."

They made their way through the village, past the monastery and the church ever climbing up the hill upon which Flaubert's castle stood. It was grand indeed and still growing. Great gates set behind a proper moat; tall towers, a huge courtyard, the enormous doors of oak with beaten iron hinges. In they walked everything was excessive. Deerhounds the size of ponies lay in the rushes covering the limestone floor; the animal's sleep belying their speed and ferocity. Servants were hurrying everywhere. They climbed the steps to the great hall and there was Flaubert on the dais in his golden chair.

He was wrapped in a padded silken robe from the east. His beard glistened with oil and there was a circlet about his head. "He looks like a king" Jude thought. His own tunic, good enough for his father's house looked shabby here.

Flaubert dipped his hands in some scented water, wiped them with a cloth, stood and extended his hand to Jude. Jude wiped his hands on the sides of his tunic before he grasped Flaubert wrist. "Merci, thank you for coming to see me," Flaubert purred. "Let us take a turn around the hall. Would you like some refreshment, a sweetmeat, something to drink, perhaps?" "Non merci, no thank you. Je suis bon." Spoke Jude hesitantly. "Ah, you speak a civilized language, I see. That is good." "My father had us learn your language, he thought it best to know the enemy" Flaubert laughed. "That at least is honest, but then most Saxons are honest, foolish, stubborn, but honest."

Jude stiffened," You wanted to see me?" Flaubert paused and looked at Jude, then he smiled. He had seen the anger, the bitterness in Jude's eyes. He knew he had a willing audience. "Soon there will be a gathering of the Saxon Lords.

Your father will go to this meeting. They wish to come to an understanding with the King. I have been trying for years to get your father to come to an understanding with me. He refuses to listen. Here is what I want from you. I need to know when your father goes to this meeting and the path he will take. You will tell me this. In return I promise to give you all your father's lands as your holding if you will acknowledge me as your liege lord. Your father will not be harmed, he will just be removed from his domain and you will take his place." "What about my brother?" Jude asked.
"One cannot have everything, unless of course you are me. I will not guarantee his safety. Times are hard, travel is dangerous. Besides, if an accident should befall your brother that would make it much easier for you to assume control of the lands. My lands in your control." "I will need some time to consider your proposal." said Jude slowly. "You may send me word within the week, but it must be soon. I know time of the gathering is near."
Jude was galloping home on his horse. He had stayed too long. What if his brother or Father asked where he had been?

But his mind kept coming back to the riches of Flaubert's house and the thought that Flaubert needed him, needed his help. He slipped in the great hall just as the evening meal was beginning.

He had not been missed. His father, Sir Barth was at the head of the table, his mother Gwenned next to him. Gawain came in and sat across from Jude. The rest of the table was filled with family retainers and distant relatives who lived on the estate. He saw himself at the head of the table, smiling and being generous to all these people.

He would be a good Lord of the Manor. Suddenly he realized his father had been speaking. "So you Jude will remain here with your mother while Gawain and I go to the gathering of the Saxon lords." Sire, when will you go?" Jude asked. "In six days the moon will be at the full. We will leave then and ride at night. We will cross the stream at the ford and head South toward Wood Leigh. It is four days ride. We two will go and one servant. The fewer people the less attention we will draw from Flaubert. If the Lord wills we shall return in a fortnight.

We must come to some agreement as Saxons and I believe we must come to some agreement with the King as well. I will gladly take him as my liege lord, swearing fealty to him. He is a good and honest man and desires Norman and Saxon to dwell together in peace." "My lord, you will be careful. You will take care?" breathed Gwenned to her husband.

"I shall take such care as can be taken; my love, but these are dangerous times." "Father, may I ride with you as far as the stream?" asked Jude. "Yes, that far you may ride, but then you must return to run the estate and protect your mother. Let us enjoy our time while we may and pray all goes well with the gathering and with the King."

The days crawled for Jude until the gathering. He had sent a message to Flaubert of the time and place of the meeting. He had told him how few would be traveling and that he would be at the stream on the night. There were times when he wished to throw himself into his father's arms and confess all. Other times when he worried over what this would do to his mother. But each time he felt the weight of his betrayal he told himself it was for the best. He would make it all right in the end. Everything would work out.

He comforted himself with the thought of how he would run the estate, of how he would improve things. He thought of Flaubert's castle and if Flaubert should become king himself. Then perhaps Jude would get a greater estate, more land, more gold, more power.

The final day came. All was in readiness. The pack horses were ladened for the journey.

His father kissed his mother farewell and mounted his horse. Gawain bade her farewell also. As he eased himself into the saddle he made sure of his sword and shifted his bow around his shoulders. Jude joined them as they set off.

The full moon turned the world silver as they rode through the fields awaiting the harvest. Soon the glow of a window and a ribbon of smoke from the chimney were the only sign that there was a manor, then as they rode on into the wood it was only the smoke. At first they spoke together, but as the night closed in about them each rider seemed encased in his own thoughts. Owls hooted in the night. The foxes barked their strange unnatural wail. The horses made little noise as they walked.

Only the occasional jingle of a bit or the creak of a saddle broke the silence.

They had been riding for some time. The plan was to reach the stream, cross it at the ford and make camp on the other side. Jude would remain with them in what was left of the night and make his way back alone in the morning. Soon they could hear the sound of the stream as they drew near. White stones marked the fording place. The horses splashed slowly across picking their way gently through the water, heads lowered.

The four travelers had reached the other side. Sir Barth was beginning to dismount when riders with torches swept down the road out of the trees. Gawain recognized Reynard in the glow of his torch. "We are betrayed, Father!" Even as he shouted he drew his bow and began to aim his arrows at the figures carrying the torches. He heard other bows singing in the night as well.

The servant with them was a powerful warrior and he roared ahead swinging his axe at the helmeted heads gleaming in the moonlight. "Jude, Jude, draw your sword and ride to Father. He is down." Gawain shouted. It was true. In the pale light of the moon, Sir Barth had been struck by an arrow even as he tried to regain his saddle. Gawain rode toward where he had seen Reynard last.

He found him as their swords flashed in the moonlight. He had seen enemies fall by his arrows. Another he struck down with his sword as he sought Reynard. They were fighting. Their swords ringing. Reynard was shouting to his men, but those who were still alive had fled under the barrage of arrows and the swinging axe. As the Norman turned to bring others to seize Sir Barth Gawain's sword went home and Reynard collapsed from his saddle.

Gawain saw the servant with his father. He knelt beside Reynard. "Who has betrayed us? Who told you we would be here? You are dying Reynard. You cannot die without honor. Tell me." Reynard gasped for breath. His hands clutched his wound.

"You must ask your little brother. He knows." And Reynard was gone, his eyes glazing over as the light went out of them.

 Gawain and the servant bound Sir Garth's wound and got him on his horse. He was weak, but he could ride. Jude was nowhere to be seen. As they crossed the stream they saw him standing with the pack horses. One look told Gawain all he needed to know. Jude was the betrayer. Jude had traded his father's life for his father's lands.

No words were spoken on the return. Even in his suffering Sir Barth also had realized his youngest son's treachery. That pierced him to his heart more than any arrow. They reached the manor. Sir Barth was placed in his bed. Gwenned saw to his wound. The under-sheriff was summoned and the great machine that was the law began to turn and Jude was caught in its embrace. There was a trial. Other Saxon lords came. The truth of the betrayal became known.

In the end the undersheriff read the sentence of the court. "The sentence for betrayal is trial by arrow. The accused will be taken to the tournament fields. He will be bound to a target. At 200 paces 6 arrows will be fired by yeomen of the estate. May the flight of the arrows be guided by the hand of justice!" The undersheriff lowered the parchment with the sentence.

"Bring him!" he growled to his yeomen. Slowly they marched to the far end of the tournament fields. Jude was bound to a wooden target, the cords biting into his wrists and ankles. The undersheriff took a rag and bound it over his eyes. Jude had begged for it. He had no desire to follow the flight of an arrow toward him. He heard the men trudge away.

Soon the horn would sound and the arrows would fly. Which one would kill him? Which one would maim him for life if it did not kill? He had witnessed these trials before. He had seen men pierced in the eye or the throat, carrying the shame of their wounds for all to see for the rest of their lives if the arrows did not kill them. Suddenly he felt a coolness close over him, and a darkness.

Perhaps the sun had gone behind a cloud, perhaps this was the calm of death. The horn sounded. "First arrow" announced the undersheriff. There was a soft twang of the bowstrings and then silence. In a moment he heard and felt the arrow strike the target beside his head.

"They were going for the kill" he thought. He had betrayed his father, his people. Death was his deserving.

The horn. "Second arrow" again the sound of the bowstrings, again the silent flight, again the sound of the arrow beside his head on the other side. "Why were they waiting? Why was it taking so long? Were they trying to draw this out, prolong the suffering, the dread? The horn "Third arrow."

This time he heard nothing until he heard a hiss nearby, a quick intake of breath, but from whom, from where? His mind was reeling. Again the call of the horn. "Fourth arrow."

His ears were straining for the sound, the flight, then he heard it. The sound of an arrow on metal. What could it be? Had someone left a shield on the ground nearby? The horn blew "Fifth arrow." Now again he heard the bow, again the silence, again the sound of the arrow striking somewhere nearby. "They were waiting. They were trying to make him think he was safe. Trying to deceive him into hope before the last arrow pierced him and he would die. Would they not hurry? Can they be so cruel? The last horn blast "Sixth arrow." Finally! The twang of the bowstrings.
"This is it, I am a dead man" he thought. Another hiss near him, another intake of breath. Suddenly the cloth covering his eyes was pulled away and he was staring into the face of his brother. Was Gawain going to kill him since the arrows had not done their work? What was the look in his eyes? Then Jude saw the blood dripping from Gawain's ear where the third arrow had left its mark.

His eyes found the arrow imbedded in Gawain's shoulder where the last flight had struck him as he held up his shield. Other hands untied him as the truth slowly dawned upon Jude. His brother had stood in his place. His brother had stood between him and the arrows, between him and his punishment. His brother had taken the arrows for him, wounded for him, shedding his blood for the betrayer. What love is this? What were the words of the Master?

"Greater love has no man than this that he lay down his life for his friend." He flung his arms around Gawain supporting his wounded arm. Gawain smiled weakly. "You will always be welcome here, you will always have my protection.   You will always be my brother. I will always love you."

He saw the disbelieving looks of others, the accusing eyes of those who knew he should have been shot. He knew that some would always carry the accusations in their heart. Some would always think of him as the betrayer. He did not care.

He knew only that his brother had put himself between Jude and death and that knowledge would be enough for him until the end of his days whatever might happen.

They made their way home to carry the news to their father still recovering from his wounds. Sir Barth was standing at the gate that led to the keep, Gwenned beside him supporting him; he worried that he might have lost both his sons in the betrayal of the one. Waiting. Waiting for the return of his sons.

How he rejoiced to have two sons again. As Gawain was now carried into the house Sir Barth turned to his wayward child and forgave him his treachery, kissed him and clasped Jude to him. The one who was lost now returned, restored, his debt paid. The betrayal expunged.

The End.

2
SERVANT OF ALL

"The sad fact is that there is evil in the world. People do bad things, mostly to each other. The only way you can defeat that is by doing good, boy and fighting the evil as best you may." Said Gareth's father. They were looking down at what was left of a deer after poachers had taken what they wanted. "It's easy to say 'everyone is doing it' and the deer are there for the taking', but that doesn't make it right."
"But what of the starving, Father?" Gareth said. "In our village we feed them.

I know there are those who through misfortune are left without proper food and clothing, but it is my duty as Lord of the Manor to help them and so we do, but this is not out of need, but to flaunt the law and for the pleasure of killing. There is too much meat left here to spoil for this to be an act of hunger. Whoever did this has taken the antlers, enough meat to roast over a fire in the moment and nothing else. See, here is the fire, left to go out on its own with no thought that it might burn down the forest and everything in it." His father said.

They were hunting together. It was still early morning. Gareth was learning to track and hunt with his father. He was learning to tell the size of the buck by the height of the antler scrapings on the trees and the weight of it by the depth of the print in the soft earth. His father was teaching him the ways of the wood as well as the ways of the world. "The foxes and stoats have had more of this deer that those who shot it. What is left is good only for the carrion beasts. This could have help feed those in the village. The hide would have been used as well. Now it is spoilt and good for nothing."

Gareth had an idea who had done this. He had heard of some of the older boys in the village bragging about a kill but they had neither the skill nor the knowledge to use the game wisely. They knew enough to kill, but not to use the benefit of what they had killed other than filling their gullets. "Anyone can destroy. Anyone can take life. Anyone can tear down." His father broke in on Gareth's thoughts. "Not everyone can build up. It's not the poaching that bothers me; it's the waste, the wanton killing."

Gareth hid his thoughts from his father because he didn't know what he should do. They hunted on with his father returning to the poached deer with mutterings erupting every now and again. The two of them came home later in the morning with one buck and a brace of rabbits. His father had shown him how to dress each of them to get the most out of the meat and hide. They bore the deer between them back to the manor house with it tilting precariously from his father's tall shoulder to his own shorter one.

The two hunters handed their bounty to the cook to prepare with his father's admonition to "see that those who are in need in the village get a portion." They shared hot cider and some bread to hold them over 'til midday.

"Get to your lessons now, Gareth, and see that you help your sister with hers." "Yes, Father." Gareth said. Gareth did not mind helping his sister, Megan. She was only six. Not quite half his age, but they were friends and although she was sometimes too faithful a follower, most of the time he did not mind. It was only when he wanted to run through the woods with his friends and pretend to attack the Norsemen invaders with wooden swords his father had made for him and she wanted to be the rescued maiden that he wished she were elsewhere.

He finished his schooling and he helped Megan with hers. Counting for six year olds was much easier than the sums his mother set for him. His father wanted him to be able to read and write, do sums and learn all that would be needed to run the estate and make his way in the world. Gareth wanted to play. He knew that he would have the rest of his life to be an adult. Time for learning was over for today.

It was fall and there were still a few apples clinging belatedly on the trees in the orchard and wild grapes to be had if you knew where to look. He found his friends from the village, Aiden and Eamon and went to the stream that ran through his father's lands. "Let's catch some fish." Eamon said. "I'm hungry."

"You are always hungry." Aiden pronounced. "Yes, well, I am! Let's go catch some fish." Eamon responded. "Let's see if there are apples first and then go to the stream" said Gareth.

Each grabbed a pole from the house and they swarmed their way through the village with the reckless energy of youth and on to the orchard at the back of the manor house. With care they searched the trees making sure not to break any branches. "Broken branches bare no fruit!" His father's forester had said over and over. Gareth was the thinnest and lightest of the three. He scrambled to the tops of the trees and found enough fruit for each of them with an extra apple for his sister for later. Eamon ate his apple, core, seeds and all but the stem. "Eamon when you eat a pig, I'll bet you even eat the squeal!" Aiden told him. "I wish I had a pig to eat right now.

I'd have him snout, ears, tail and the squeal too all roasted and ready to go." "Of course with that apple in your mouth you sort of look like a pig. Snort, snort." Aiden teased. "I'll show you a pig, you squirrel!" With that Eamon tackled his friend and they rolled on the ground until Gareth pulled them apart his wiry strength getting the better of the two sturdier boys. "Enough you two! You'll do that 'til one of you gets mad and then it won't be fun anymore." Gareth was ever the peacemaker between his friends.

They found themselves down by the stream, its gentle bubbling blending with the sound of dry leaves clinging still on the trees stirred by the fall breeze. Aiden began turning over rocks looking for something to bait the bone hooks tied with twine at the ends of their rods. It didn't take long for the three of them to put their baited lines in the water waiting for the fish to strike.

"We saw a poached deer in the forest this morning." Gareth said. "Father said it was wasteful to kill the deer and not take all the meat. I think he could forgive the poaching because he says people need to eat, but the waste made him very angry."

Aiden and Eamon looked at each other across the stream. They knew who had killed the deer. Brant had boasted of it to his friends and the news had spread quickly through the youth of the village. Brant was the bully of the village and the biggest of all the boys. "I know that Brant did it." Gareth had seen the look his friends had exchanged. "But I didn't say anything."

"You'd better not, Gareth. Brant would hurt you, Lord's son or not." Aiden said. Aiden had a temper that often got him into trouble, but he was afraid of Brant.

"Yes, well he may be able to bash me, but something needs to be done." At that moment Eamon's line tightened and his pole dipped under the weight of a fish. "I've got one!" "Bring him in! Bring him in! The other boys shouted. Eamon began backing up pulling the fish after him; keeping the line taut and the pole tip up as his father had taught him. The water had exploded with the fish fighting to free itself from the line, but Eamon kept the fish on the line pulling it to shore.

Gareth and Aiden were shouting over and over "Bring him in! Careful now! Watch out or you'll lose him!" Finally Eamon got the fish to the water's edge and landed him on the shore.

The fish was flopping about flashing his silver sides, his mouth opening in great gulps. "It's a tench!" Said Gareth. "He's no good. You must have let your line hit the bottom." Aiden told him. "He's no good. He's a rough fish." "He'll eat in some stew with potatoes and carrots." Said Eamon as he picked up a rock and hit the fish in the head stilling its struggles. Eamon's family had a small freehold on the edge of the village. They kept bees and farmed.

Eamon wrapped the fish in the grasses by the stream to keep it and started looking for more bait under the rocks and fallen limbs by the stream. Just then the other two boys had fish take their lines almost pulling the rods from their hands while they were distracted. Each landed their fish, a fierce pike for Gareth and a fat sunfish for Aiden. Gareth broke a willow branch from the water willow and threaded it through the fish's gills. He looped the branch around, put the fish back in the water and weighted the branch with a rock.

"That will keep them fresh until we go. Hopefully the pike can't eat the sunfish like that. Eamon, you can have my catch." Gareth knew that Eamon's family did not have much, freehold or not.

Aiden's father was a shepherd for Gareth's family and his mother was the manor cook. The boys fished until dusk. Then they headed home for the evening meal. They'd caught more fish, enough for Eamon's family to make a good meal and even enough for Eamon's hunger to be abated for the night.

After the evening meal Gareth sat by the fire in the great hall with his father and mother. They each talked about their own plans and news for the day. Gareth was stroking Akela, the deer hound that was always to be found by his mother's side. He loved the size of the hound. It was almost too big to be real. The beast was bigger than he was, but as gentle as a lamb with the family, ferocious as a bear with anyone else. Akela had put up with him and his sister as they had treated her as toy, horse, pillow and playmate over the years. "Father" said Gareth hesitantly. "I know who killed the deer."

"Ah. I thought you might. But you don't want to tell me because that would be telling, right?" His father said quietly. "Yes, Father." "Well, I don't think its Aiden or Eamon. It's not Oswin, Ryce or Treddian, so I'm thinking its Brant and his two minions, Kale and Bren." Gareth looked up startled into his father's face. "How did you know?"

"Well, if I didn't before your face has just told me, but I also know the village and the boys in it. Brant is a troubled soul. He's big. He's not the brightest brand in the fire, but he has cunning. And I know things are not going well in his home. His father drinks almost as much mead as they sell at the inn and when he drinks he is a mean man. I have known Brant's mother all her life. She grew up here in the village inheriting the inn from her father. She married outside of the village to a man she met at a passing spring fair and now she suffers for her choice. She knows I know and she knows we care. She also knows that if she needs help we will help her, but if she does not ask then I will not interfere. As for Brant himself, I do not know. What do you think I should do?"

"Eldred that is hardly a fair question for your son" Ardith said. "I just want him to think about it. That is all. Being the Lord of the Manor is not always pleasant. There are hard choices that must be made." "Yes, but he doesn't have to make them now." His mother replied. "He will one day, God willing. Think on it, Gareth. Let me know what is in your thoughts."

Gareth lay awake long into the night, his mind churning over and over about what he should do. Finally he drifted into sleep. He awoke with no more an idea than he had when he had fallen asleep.

The day began as always with chores and lessons. When all was completed he found his friends and their wanderings began again. Not fishing today, but warriors ranging through the forests fighting the fierce invaders from Denmark. The three friends had slain seven Norse bushes and captured three Norse holly trees when they came on another deer carcass in the wood. The three boys looked silently down at the mutilated body of a doe. It was hacked about and a shoulder haunch taken but the rest left for the flies, the fox and the buzzards. "Should we bury it?" Asked Eamon.

"Why do that?" "I don't know!" "Leave it" said Gareth.

"At least the scavengers will get something out of it. It's not good for anything else." They could see the ragged hole the arrow had made in the side of the deer. "She must have run a long way after she was shot. That would make the meat tough" said Gareth.

"How do you know?" Asked Aiden. "See the blood trail? Let's follow it." With Gareth leading, the other two boys followed him watching as he pointed out the signs his father had told him to look for in tracking. "Here's a splash of blood and here another." He said as they move. "Here she stumbled. See the way the ground is disturbed. Here's more blood." They followed the trail through the wood a long bow shot until they found a place where the leaves were churned up. "This is where she was shot. She took off and two, no, three followed her. Here are their tracks." The three boys followed the trail back to the deer now looking for the tracks of the three poachers.

"Let's look for a fire." "Why?" Said Aiden.

"When my father and I found the buck yesterday there was a fire nearby where they cooked the meat and ate it. I just think they may have done the same thing again."

They returned to the deer and cast about separately in ever widening circles around the body until Eamon called to them. "Here! I found it." There again were the remains of a small fire and places where three people had sat on the ground. "Now what?" Said Eamon. "Now we go home," said Gareth.

"Are you going to tell your father, Gareth?" "Yes. I'll have to. This must be stopped." "Why? It's not hurting anybody." Said Eamon. "Doesn't seem to do much for the deer!" Retorted Aiden. "They don't look too happy about it." Gareth smiled a crooked smile. "Because it's not right. It's poaching and it's wasteful. It's destruction for destruction's sake and that hurts all of us." The other two boys hung their heads more in worry about what might happen to their friend than anything else. The three turned for home. All of them were quiet now wrapped in their own thoughts.

As they sat at evening table finishing the meal Gareth cleared his throat and spoke, "Father, we found another deer in the forest today. It was the same as before, a small portion taken and the rest left to rot." "What do you think I should do, son?" "Well, we don't have proof of who's doing this even though we think we know. If you go to Brant's father he will just beat him and that won't make Brant any better just more determined not to get caught."

"If you go to Brant he may just deny it and then you will have to do something about it or look foolish in the village." "You are right enough there, son." His father said. "But it must be stopped before other louts begin to do the same and there will be no more of King Alfred's deer in the forest. What you have said so far is good. Keep thinking about it. Off to bed with you now. I love you. Sleep well."

Again Gareth lay awake for a while thinking of what he might do. "I must follow Brant and catch him in the act." With that firmly in his mind Gareth made a plan. He would get his chores and lessons done as quickly as he could, take Akela with him and try to follow Brant and his band of louts into the woods.

He awoke early and put his plan into action. He raced through his chores and his lessons with vigor if not with accuracy. His tutor wondered what was wrong with him. When Aiden and Eamon arrived Gareth told them his plan and they wanted to join him, but he persuaded them that one could move more silently thorough the woods than three and so they left him reluctantly alone.

"You watch you don't get caught, Gareth." Eamon had warned. "Brant would kill you. He's that mean."

First Brant and his minions had to be found. Gareth walked slowly through the village with Akela by his side. He went down the back lane behind the inn to see if he could see or hear Brant by the scullery. He was peering into the gloom of the doorway when he heard a voice from within. "What're ye looking at, young whelp? Think you see something do you?" It was Brant's father, Malburn. Gareth recognized the slurred speech of someone who was drunk. He couldn't see the man in the dark of the room. "Think you're better'n me? Better'n all of us?" He began to see movement in the darkness as the figure approached the sunshine streaming in at the doorway.

Malburn was massive, frightening. "Go on with you! Get out of it!" As Malburn drew into the light Gareth could see he had a clay jug in his hand. "Sorry, sir" Gareth said. Akela let out a low growl and then a deep bark that set the man back and almost sobered him for a moment. "Aaaah! Don't set your rabid hound on me!" Malburn screamed and staggered back into the gloom. Gareth strode quickly off with Akela beside him. "Good girl! Good girl!"

He said as he stroked her head and walked along. But he still had not found Brant. Gareth made his way to the edge of the village near Eamon's family's holding. He had just entered the cover of the wood when he heard voices nearby.

"Let's see if we can make another kill today!" Said Brant. "It's too soon." Kale replied. "If the foresters find too many dead deer Eldred will alert the High Sheriff and they will start hunting for us and they know how to track." "That's part of the fun. Getting away with it. That and the killing and the eating afterwards." Brant growled. "Now, who's with me?" The two other boys silently assented. They knew better than to cross Brant. They had seen his temper and felt his fists.

Gareth overheard all this and was grimly delighted. He would stalk them and catch them in the act although like the story of the man who caught the wolf by the ears, he wasn't sure what he would do when he caught them. The older boys set out at a loping pace that carried them quickly into the heart of his father's wood. Gareth and Akela set off silently behind them at a distance.

The boys were easy to follow because of the speed they were going and the tracks they made through the wood. As they got deeper into the trees the older boys slowed and began to cast about on the deer trails for their quarry. Even Brant knew enough to get downwind of his prey so that he could ease himself closer to his target.

Now they were stepping carefully and quietly looking for the horizontal lines that would catch their eye. They were looking for small movements, an ear flicking, a head bobbing down to forage. Gareth and Akela were going slower still. Gareth was worried that Akela would growl or bark, but her training held good and she was as silent as he as they went along.

Gareth was close enough to see the other boys now or rather he could see two of them, Brant's followers, Kale and Bren but not Brant. He must be working himself into a better position to shoot a deer as the others drove the animal along by their presence. Gareth felt something in his hair and his hand went up instinctively to brush it away. It was tree bark.

He looked up to see Brant's wide grinning face high above him in a Black Poplar. Brant dropped a fist sized stone that caught Akela in the head and knocked her down. Brant yelled and fell on Gareth with his heavy body. Gareth cried out and went down under Brant's weight. He was trapped and breathless under Brant's bulk. "Stalk me, you skulking little ferret! I'll teach you to follow me, you weasel, you stoat!" Brant was slapping and punching him about the face until finally with one great blow to the side of Gareth's head everything went black. When Gareth came to he was lying next to Akela. He could see the dried blood that oozed from the gash made by the stone, but he could also see her rib cage going up and down in regular breaths. She was still alive.

He tried to move himself, but found he was trussed up like a pheasant bound hand and foot, hands behind him, with rough twine. He could imagine the older boys laughing as they tied him up once they got over the fear that they had killed him, but would they leave him here to die in the wood? He rolled over and tried to sit up.

He felt something shift in his side, a rib. The sharp pain brought sweat to his brow. Brant and his friends must have kicked him for good measure after he blacked out for ruining their afternoon's sport. With pain tearing at his side, he worked his hands under him and brought his legs through the loop of his arms and got his hands in front of him. Gareth began to look about for something to cut the twine. He had come out without his bow and arrows and his knife was missing from its sheath; his father's gift, stolen. His eyes fell on the rock Brant had thrown at Akela. It was quartz and had sharp edges. Gareth maneuvered himself around so he could grasp the rock with his tied hands. He placed it between his knees and squeezed tight. Then he began rubbing the twine on the jagged edge of the white stone.

His legs started to ache with holding the stone tightly between his knees and the rough twine was rubbing his wrists raw, but he kept going. Finally the twine parted and he untied his ankles. He was free, but he couldn't leave Akela.

She was still breathing, but she had made no move to get up and her eyes were still closed. Gareth stroked her side and spoke to her softly, "It's all right now. It's all right now. Easy girl. Good dog." There were tears in his eyes for his friend. Carefully Gareth got up holding his side and walked slowly around to get his bearings. He could see by the sun he hadn't been out too long.

The hurried tracks of his tormentors headed off toward the village. The sun was setting; night was coming. He couldn't just leave Akela here alone for any nocturnal predators that might come along. He would have to carry her home. She weighed more than he did, at least a hundred weight. He got down on his knees, ducked his head next to her belly and began pulling her dead weight over his head to the back of his neck. Akela gave a soft whimper as he gently moved her. When he bent over the pain was awful.

With Akela draped over him he got his hands under him and pushed himself up. He rocked back on his heels now almost falling backward with her weight. He got one leg under him and then the other in a crouch. He took a deep breath and forced himself to stand upright with the dog draped around his shoulders like a lamb, only this was more like a sheep and a large one at that. His side was burning.

He turned toward the setting sun and began to make his way through the forest back to the manor house. With every step he felt the weight of Akela. His legs and back were shaking with the strain. It was not long before he was breathing heavily, deep chest heaving breaths as he struggled along; a searing stab with every breath. Sweat poured down his face and in his eyes. He knew it wasn't just from the exertion but from the pain as well.

Suddenly over the sound of his breathing he heard the noise of someone moving through the forest, disturbing the bracken. He had stopped to rest leaning his back against a tree. His eyes scanned the distance trying to find the source of the noise in the gloom. What if it were Brant and his followers coming back to finish him or continue their sport with him?

He was too exhausted to run and he would not leave Akela to them. The noise grew closer. Then he heard voices.

"How are we going to find him in the dark?" Aiden asked. "I don't know "answered Eamon. "We'll just keep looking." "Over here!" Gareth croaked. He could hardly speak and the shout had taken all his breath. He stood leaning against the tree waiting for the two friends to come to him. "You're alive!" Exclaimed Eamon. "So far" Gareth answered. "We weren't sure what we would find" said Aiden. "We overheard Brant bragging about what he had done. His friends were that scared. They thought you might be dead." "Anyway, when we heard him we thought we could just come looking for you" said Eamon. "I'm glad you did" rasped Gareth. "Aiden, head back and ask your father to come. Ask him to bring something to bear Akela. He's taken care of enough sheep; maybe he'll know what to do for Akela. Please ask him to hurry." Aiden took off through the woods winding his way through the trees. "Help me put her down, please, Eamon."

Slowly Gareth sank to his knees with Eamon steadying him. He reversed the process of getting Akela on his shoulders and Eamon helped easing the unconscious animal over Gareth's head. Gareth stroked her again and spoke softly to her in his soothing voice. There was a another small whimper from Akela.

It wasn't long before the two boys heard footsteps hurrying through the woods. Aiden had returned with his father and a small sledge that his father used for moving injured sheep. Eilert sucked his breath through his teeth when he saw Akela. He was a kind man and a good shepherd. "Will she be all right?" Gareth asked. "Time will tell, son. Time will tell. We'll get her home and by a warm fire. Dog's don't hurt like we do, but this is quite a wound. We'll get her safe home and then it may just be a matter of waiting to see if time and her own body will do its work. I'll put a poultice on her and we'll make her comfortable. Then we'll see. What about you? You're looking none too good yourself." The shepherd said. "I think they've cracked a rib. The rest is just bruising" said Gareth. "If I move slowly it doesn't hurt too much." "Well then, let's head back."

The four of them made their way slowly through the woods, occasionally lifting the sledge over a rough place to keep from jostling Akela any more than was necessary, sometimes waiting for Gareth to catch his breath. Finally they reached the manor.

"We'll take her to the kitchen and put her by the fire there. It is never out and that way there will be someone to watch her." He put his hand on Gareth's shoulder. "Don't fret over this, boy. Akela is a good strong dog in her prime. Time may heal this, but if not it is better that it was her head and not yours. Do you understand?" "Yes, sir." Gareth did understand, but that didn't make him any happier to know he might lose his friend.

The three others left after making Akela comfortable on a pallet by the fire. The scullion who turned the spit and kept the fire looked at Gareth. "It's better than it looks. Not a word, understand?" The young boy just nodded and looked down. Gareth tried to catch his reflection in a bucket of water there in the kitchen. He could see dark patches of dried blood and his eye was swollen almost shut. There was a long cut on his cheek where Brant's foot had caught him.

He would have to clean up before his parents saw him. "What happened to your face?" It was his sister, Megan. "I had a little trouble." "Mama says I'm a little trouble sometimes. Did I do that to your face?" "No, Megan. Mama was just teasing you, but this isn't funny. Please don't say anything about it to anyone." "I won't have to say anything, Gareth. They can see it on your face." He smiled and began to wash off the blood and dab at the edges of the cut on his cheek. There was another on his forehead he felt when he splashed the water to his face. "I must look grim."

He started to laugh, but then he felt the rib when he took a deep breath and stopped with a cough. He was nearly finished when his mother came in to check on the preparations for supper and saw him. "What has happened?" Ardith asked falling to her knees and embracing him. A sharp intake of breath made her stop, sit back and take Gareth by the shoulders. "What is wrong? Did you fall? I don't need to ask if you are hurt. That I can see. Where are you hurt?"

"Just a little fall in the wood, Mother" Gareth said lightly.

Sweat broke out on his forehead again from the pain and his face turned ashen from her initial embrace. The fear and excitement had carried him this far, but now the pain was overwhelming him. "I think something's wrong with my rib. Nothing else though, well except for my face and maybe my arms and legs." Fear, anger, love and frustration poured out of her heart. "What were you doing? What were you thinking? What has happened?" The words tumbled out of her in a rush. Now she was shaking, trying to remain calm. He decided to tell her. "I was following those Father thinks are poaching the deer and I got caught. They hit Akela with a rock and then knocked me out. I think they kicked me in the ribs and a few other places. I woke up and tried to get back with Akela. Aiden and Eamon found me. Aiden's father came and we all made it back here. I feel like a fool."

Ardith remained silent for a long time and Gareth thought she was going to cry and then he thought she might berate him herself. "Let's clean you up and see to your rib." She decided her son had done a very adult thing albeit a foolish one and should be treated accordingly.

She got a cloth and cleaned his face catching the places he had missed. Then she got some lanolin salve with comfrey and put it on the cuts. "Take off your jerkin and your shirt."

"I don't think I can raise my arms, Mother." Gareth said. Then the tears began to flow in Ardith's eyes. She unlaced the leather jerkin and eased it off his shoulders. Then she took his left sleeve and held the cuff as Gareth slid his arm slowly out of it. She did the same with the right sleeve but with considerably more pain on his part as he moved his arm out of the sleeve. There he stood naked to the waist. She could see clearly the depression in the rib cage where the rib was displaced. There would be bruising later, but now his pale flesh was unmarked. All this time the kitchen had continued to operate around them as if nothing were happening. The scullion continued to turn the spit over the fire; the cook kept up her perpetual motion from cauldron to fire to table and back again. They were in the still center of a hive of activity. His mother sent one of the serving girls to fetch some cloth from the housekeeper. When she returned Ardith took the linen fabric, nicked it with her own small jeweled dagger and began to rip it into strips.

She placed the end on his left side. "Hold this." She said and began to wrap the wide bands slowly, carefully around his thin torso. "This will support the ribs until they heal. It will also keep you from moving too much. You will need to be careful not to twist or bend any more than you must, lest the rib pierces the lung and then you will die." She said all this very calmly and matter of fact even as the tears rolled from her eyes. "I have bandaged the wounded in my time and never thought to do so again, certainly not my own son, but you are growing up and I should have expected this."

"What about Father?" The quaver in Gareth's voice belied his calm. "I will tell him you are injured. You will get to bed. I will bring you some supper. You can tell him in the morning after a night's sleep." "What about Akela?" Gareth asked "She will be cared for here in the kitchen. Time will tell." His mother said.

He went to his room and got into bed. His mother brought him some hot broth and bread. "Here, drink this." "What is it?" "Juice of the poppy, it will help you sleep." He did as he was told and soon he was sleeping peacefully.

Gareth roused once in the small hours and saw his father's form stretched out on the floor beside his bed. Gareth closed his eyes again and drifted off again.

It was the pain that woke him in the morning. His head hurt, his jaw, his eye, his ribs, his legs all bore the marks of Brant's attentions. He tried to sit up, but the pain wracked his body and he eased back onto the mattress with a hiss and a small groan. In his short young life he had never known such pain. The thought slowly grew within, "Is this what Brant feels when his father beats him?"

Gareth slowly eased on his side and began to swing his legs out from under the woolen blankets that covered his thin body. He could see under his nightshirt his legs were mottled deep purple with tinges of greenish yellow. He knew the rest of him would look the same. His father had awakened early and was about his own work with only a folded blanket to show he had ever been there. He took the blanket and wrapped it slowly about his shoulders.

He felt the cold of morning in his weakened body and was shivering slightly. He stood by the brazier that heated his room and let the warmth work through his body. He didn't hurt any less, but the heat felt good.

A servant had heard his waking groans and soon his mother was knocking at his door. "Gareth, may I come in?" His mother asked in her clear warm voice. "Yes, Mother." He croaked. She opened the door and Kiva, Aiden's mother, followed her in with a wooden tray laden with food. Golden butter swam in the middle of thick oat porridge. There was a small jug of what he knew to be honey from Eamon's father and hot cider to drink.

"Aiden was after asking if you were still alive, young master and so I brought this up myself." Gareth smiled through the pain and thanked her for the food. She set the tray on the bed, bobbed gracefully and went out. He made his way back to bed and his mother helped him sit up with a pillow at his back. She placed the tray in his lap. He bowed his head in silent thanks for the food and began to eat. Ardith stood watching his slow painful movements. He was eating with his left hand.

Raising his right to his lips was too painful with his broken rib. Finally he put the horn spoon down. It took too much out of him. "Would you like some help?" "Please." She sat beside him and began to feed him. "You won't need to make noises and open your mouth like you did for Megan when she was a baby." "For you too when you were a baby! But no I won't do that. Here."

She placed a napkin under his chin and dipped the spoon in the porridge. "Could I have a bit more honey, please, Mother?" "It won't sweeten you any." She teased. "No, but it does taste good." She held the mug to his lips so he could drink the cider and wiped his mouth when he was done. "Better this morning?" "The warmth feels good. I'm still having trouble getting a deep breath, and I hurt all over but everything seems to be in working order."

"Except your brain, young one." His father said as he entered the room. "What were you thinking going against those three alone? You could have been killed." His voice was shaking with emotion. "I didn't plan on getting caught. How is Akela?" Gareth asked.

At that moment the deer hound came quietly into the room. She came up to him and licked his face. He reached out slowly to touch her feeling her warmth through her wiry coat. She sniffed at him and then lay down by the brazier with her head on her paws.

"She's moving slowly, but otherwise fine, no thanks to you." Said his father. His mother sat silently through this exchange. She knew how distraught her husband was over what had happened . . . over what might have happened. They both knew it was a miracle that this conversation was taking place and not a wake for their impetuous son.

"We were tracking the three of them through the forest. I thought if I could catch them poaching; see them in the act then I could tell you and you would have a witness and you would know what to do. I didn't think I would get hurt."

"Just stop with 'I didn't think!' and go on from there. Do you know what your mother's been through? What I have been through? Do you know what went through our minds when you couldn't be found for supper and then when we heard what had happened? You could have been killed. We might have lost you."

Hot tears were brimming in his father's eyes as he stood there with the emotion of the moment filling him. "I am sorry. I truly didn't think about getting hurt. I didn't think about how you might feel if I did. But one thing I have thought about is how Brant must feel. If his father beats him like he hit me he must feel this way a lot. It's no wonder he gets angry and wants to kill something."

"I'll have to think about that one myself, young man. Get some rest and I'll come see you later." Gareth's father went out of the room. His mother gathered up the tray, set it aside and began to tuck him in with the covers. "Try to sleep some more." She gave him a few more drops of poppy juice. "Let your body heal itself. Akela will keep you company." And so Gareth slept the rest of the day away and most of the next day; waking only to eat a little. His body was healing although the bruising looked worse each day. Finally on the fourth day he felt much better, enough to get up and take a few steps around his room. "I feel like Lazarus, Mother, in the story from the Bible." "You smell like him too, remember his sister said, 'Lord surely he stinketh. He hath been dead four days."

"I'll bring up some hot water and you can wash here by the brazier."

After his wash-up Gareth did feel better. His mother came back in before he put his tunic on to wrap his ribs again. He still needed help with anything that required raising his arms above his head. Gareth spent a few more days around the manor house before his father or mother would let him venture outside. At the end of the day Eamon and Aiden had come to see him and they had played together indoors, the unasked questions hanging there in the air among them, "Where was Brant? What was he doing?" Finally Eamon broached the subject.

"I heard Brant's two friends have deserted him. What he did to you scared them so badly they've vowed to have no more to do with him." He said this between bites of the plate of scones and fig preserves Keva, Aiden's mother, had set for them to eat as they sat together. "These are good!" He said. "How would you know, you great lout? They don't stay on your tongue long enough to taste them." Aiden said. "You shovel them down faster than either of us can reach for another one." "I'm hungry." "You are always hungry!" Both the other boys said together.

"Anyway," he said licking the preserves from his fingers, "his friends are staying away from him, but he still goes out hunting by himself."

"That is foolish, what if something happened to him?" said Gareth. "What you mean like someone found him, tied him up beat him and left him for dead, that kind of foolish?"

"I already got that lecture from my father; I don't need another one from you, Aiden."

"When can you go out?" Eamon asked, changing the subject.

"Next week if the physician says my ribs are healed. He comes in and pokes and prods me every so often." answered Gareth. "Harvest is nearly finished and winter is coming on. We should still have some fine days to go about in." "Oh we know all about harvest. We've bound wheat into sheaves until our arms were falling off!" said Aiden. "Some of us have to work, you know. We're not all lay-about sons of the Lord of the Manor." Replied Eamon. This was the way they spoke among themselves. If things got too serious between them they would always throw this at him, knowing he felt very conscious of his position.

Gareth threw the last scone at Eamon who caught it and popped it in his mouth with a smile. "Thanks!" He mumbled with his mouth full of scone and the crumbs on his lips.

Gareth continued to sleep, sit by the fire in the great hall and hobble about the manor house wrapped in the woolen cloak his mother had made for him on her loom. His lessons continued with his tutor. His sister would join him; playing in her way, looking up at him from time to time as if to make sure he was still there. Megan didn't understand what had happened to her brother, only that he was not feeling well. Akela never left his side. By the time he was ready to go out and about again it was November and he had long tired of the manor house and its grounds.

Gareth would go out with Eamon and Aiden day after day. At first the activity tired him, but soon his energy of old returned and they were racing about the manor holdings, climbing trees, chasing each other through the barns and making a nuisance of themselves. One November afternoon when the work was finished for the day, Gareth said, "Let's go into the forest." Eamon and Aiden said, "No!" so quickly that it made Gareth laugh.

"What is wrong with the two of you?" "We can't go into the forest." said Aiden.

"And why not?" Gareth asked. "We didn't want to tell you. Brant's father beat him and threw him out after what he did to you. There were words. The whole village could hear them."

"And then" Eamon added, "Brant threw some things together and ran off into the forest. No one has seen him since." "He's living there like some hermit or highwayman." "We should find him." said Gareth. "No we should not!" The two other boys answered together. "We'll see." answered Gareth.

The two boys went back to their homes and Gareth made his way back to the manor house for the evening meal. He was eating well and moving easily now. The pain and the bruises long forgotten.

"Brant has fled to the forest, Father."

"I know." His father said. "I've given word for the woodsmen to look for him, but not to track him. Just to keep a look out."

"Is he . . . was he hurt? I heard about the beating his father gave him."

"I've no idea." Gareth's father said, "But he was well enough to take himself off to the wood."

"Do you know where he is, Father?"

"No and I don't want you to look for him either."

"What if he's hurt? What if he has injuries like mine?"

"Then he brought them on himself. I find little in my heart to care for one who has hurt you as he did. He got himself in to these troubles. Let him get himself out. Now to bed with you."

Gareth lay awake long into the night thinking about Brant and what he should do. His father had said he didn't want him looking for him, but he hadn't actually said not to look for Brant so trying to find him wasn't exactly disobeying his father . . . but it wasn't obeying either.

Gareth's eyes opened slowly. It was early, earlier than he usually woke. He lay for a moment savoring the warmth of the covers, knowing the room would be cold until he stirred the brazier up and got it glowing again. He splashed water in his face from his ewer and dressed quickly and silently.

He pulled on his hide boots, wrapped himself in his cloak and grabbed his bow. He slid his old knife into the side of his boot and slipped silently from the house. The gray day was just dawning with the smoke from the village fires mixing with the early fog. There were a few windows glowing with the lamp light. He made his way quickly through the village and into the wood.

There was a shallow cave deep in the woods by waterfall that would provide shelter and water for someone hiding in the wood. He would make his way there and see if he could find Brant. He had been so intent on getting away that he did not notice until he was in the wood itself that he was not alone. Akela was with him. In the misty morning light the wood was magical. Gareth could hear the birds scratching in the bracken. In the distance a fox barked its eerie cry.

The ground was damp and the leaves silent as he wove his way through the trees heading toward the cave. Akela moved silently beside him, a step behind, walking lightly for an animal so large. Her sharp nose raising from time to time to catch the air. They moved ever closer to the depths of the wood toward the cave and the falls. It took an hour of steady walking to make their way there.

Gareth could hear the water long before he could see it. He could picture it in his mind; the water cascading over the top falling forty feet to the pool below. There he and his friends has played and swam last summer; the warmth of the day only a memory now in the coming winter. In the middle of the pool was a large boulder. The cave was the hollow made by the absence of the stone that had dislodged in some distant flood. There was a steep ravine carved out by the water that fell away to the grotto below with the pool and the stone. He eased himself to the edge of the ravine. Already he had smelled the smoke of Brant's fire or someone's fire. As he scanned the entrance to the cave from the ravine's edge Brant came hobbling out, bent almost double from his injuries.

His eyes were swollen, his arm in a crude sling around his neck. Brant's father had beaten him badly; far worse than anything Brant had meted out to Gareth. Gareth looked for an approach to the cave. He moved silently downstream until he found a place to ford dry shod.

He had no desire to be wet on such a cold day with the threat of snow in the air. He picked his way over the stones to the other side of the stream; Akela padding softly behind him.

He worked his way quietly until he was within ten feet of Brant, the noise of his approach hidden by the waterfall. "Brant," he called. "Are you hurt? Do you need help?" Brant started at the voice and pulled a knife from his belt, Gareth's knife.

"What do you want? Come to kill me? Come to gloat? Get away from me. I'll kill you!"

"I just wanted to make sure you are all right."

"What do you care?" With that Brant lunged toward Gareth with the knife. Akela growled and barked loudly. She threw herself at Brant. Brant went down, struck his head on a stone and pitched into the frigid water.

Akela barked after him. Gareth shed his bow and cloak and waded in the pool to the place where Brant had gone under. Gareth was up to his neck and still couldn't feel Brant. He took a breath, a breath that the icy water nearly took away and dived down into the blackness. Nothing. He got another breath and went under again. This time he felt something, Brant's hair floating in the swirling water beneath the falls. Gareth's hand clutched the hair and with his lungs crying out for air, kicked off the bottom and to the surface. He took a great gulp of air as he came up and pulling Brant's head above the water he struggled to the shore. Brant's limp body was heavy. Gareth hooked his hands under Brant's arms and began tugging him out of the water. They had to get to the fire. He had to make sure Brant was breathing, alive. Slowly, agonizingly they inched along. Akela was barking at him trying to hurry him.

Gareth turned Brant on his side. Brant began to cough up water. His face wracked with pain with every involuntary gasp and cough. Gareth was shivering. The fear that had carried him alone began ebbing away with the chill.

He kept pulling Brant along toward the fire. He found a worn blanket and threw it over Brant elevating his head with some cast off clothing. Gareth was hurrying here and there, putting more wood on the fire, building it up, then tugging Brant closer. Gareth's lips were blue with cold and he couldn't feel his hands. His rib was reminding him it was newly mended. At last Gareth got Brant to the fire. Gareth stood shivering in his wet clothes wrapped in the dry cloak he had thrown off, thankful for its warmth.

He found his knife on the ground by the stream where Brant had dropped it when he fell. Gareth reached under his tunic and cut away part of his shirt to use as a bandage on Brant's head wound. He wrung the water out of it and wrapped it around Brant's head. It colored quickly with Brant's blood, but it staunched the bleeding.

He began to look around at Brant's camp. It was survival at its most basic and base. Rabbit bones were scattered about the fire with a few fish spines, Brant not having much patience for fishing. There was a sleeping place of sorts and very little else.

Steam began to rise from Gareth as the fire dried his sodden clothes. The cold was seeping with the water from his body; the warmth working its way in to his bones. He fetched the small bundle he had thrown down when he went in after Brant. He took a long pull from the jug of cider; some bread and hard cheese from which he tore a chunk of each with his teeth, not bothering with the knife. Brant was still unconscious, but breathing better now, not coughing.

What to do? He couldn't leave Brant. Akela would not leave him to fetch his father. He would just have to wait and make the best of it 'til someone came for him. He smiled grimly in the comfort that unlike Brant, someone would come for him. The thought wrapped itself around him in its own warmth like a cloak. He could survive for a night. He just hoped that Brant would survive as well. Gareth thought he might as well keep moving. He began to gather firewood in an ever widening circle around the camp. He found a large fallen limb he could feed into the fire as it burned down. That would keep him going for a while. It was all he could manage to drag it up along the bank.

Gareth began to talk out loud to Akela, "What if no one comes today or can't find us in the dark." "We'll just have to make the best of it, right Akela?" He wasn't sure why he was talking aloud, but it did make him feel better to say it. "Right Akela?" Akela came over to him and he scratched her behind her ears. He didn't have to lean down to do that, she was so big. Gareth looked around him once again. The clouds were covering the winter sun of late afternoon and the smell of snow was in the air.

"I'll have to get Brant under the shelter of the cave, Akela and we need a place to sleep." With that he made his way to the end of the ravine where the cut leveled out with the rest of the forest. There were a few young cedars standing like green spires in the greyness of the forest. With his knife he began to strip them of their branches.

The sharp needles pricked his hands, but the cedar would keep them off the cold earth of the cave floor and smell nice too. He made several trips back and forth until he was satisfied with the pallet he had made. He took the scattered sacking and clothing Brant had about the cave and spread it out over the cedar.

Then he once again took Brant under the arms and began to drag him toward the palate. He got him beside it rolled the unconscious lump over and over until Brant was now on his side at the far edge of the cedar bed. The smell wafted up through the sacking and Gareth gave a thought that it smelled much better than Brant after a few days in the wood. He took another bundle of old clothing and wedged it behind Brant so he would stay on his side. Gareth found the sling Brant had used, dipped in the stream and wrung it out several times. He eased his own bandage off Brant's head and replaced it with the new one.

Then he washed out the strips from his shirt and laid them out to use later. Gareth took another pull at the cider and ate more bread and cheese. He dug deeper into his bag and found one of the shriveled apples he had put in from the manor larder and bit into its aged sweetness. Now he had found his hunger bread, cheese and an apple no matter how sweet wasn't going to satisfy him. "Fish" he said aloud, "I'll catch some fish. I hope I'll catch some fish. What have I got to use?" Now he wished he had brought one of the poles from home instead of his bow. His bow! He could use his bow!

He unstrung the bow and unraveled the threads from a piece of sacking until he had more line. A hook. He looked at the detritus of Brant's camp and saw some smaller bird bones he could use to fashion a hook. This took a bit of time but using his knife and a rock to hone a point that would hook a fish he began turning over small stones to find bait that was always there. He cast his line into the stream letting it drift through the channels where he knew trout would be waiting.

He just hoped they were as hungry as he was because he didn't fancy eating the grubs he had just tossed to them. It took several tries but finally there was a tug on his line and in his fear that the fish would get away from his make-work rig he yanked the trout clear of the water on his first pull and it flopped on the bank 'til Gareth could hit it with the hilt of his knife and gut it. He spitted it on a stick and angled it over a glowing part of the fire where it could cook. Akela had watched all this in seemingly patient silence until she apparently decided she too was hungry and went off in search of her own food.

About the time Gareth's fish was cooked Akela wandered into the firelight with a rabbit in her jaws and sat down regally to eat it between her paws. Gareth continued to check on Brant. His breathing was steady and his color had returned. Gareth didn't know what else to do for him except make sure Brant was as comfortable as he could make him. Gareth grasped the stick he used to spit the fish and began to pick at the hot flesh and crispy skin with his fingers, savoring each bite. Akela looked at him. "What? You had your rabbit. Did you offer me any? No you did not!"

Akela dropped her head back down and sighed the deep sigh dogs sigh when hope is lost. Gareth tossed her a small piece of the fish which she snapped out of the air. Soon Gareth himself sigh a great sigh because his hunger was assuaged. He washed the fish from his hands in the stream and scooped some water to his mouth.

Snow began to fall. He could see the great white flakes illuminated by the fire as they drifted down and disappeared in the heat with a small hiss. This might make it harder for him, for them, to be found.

He drank more water, fed the fire to keep it going and eased into the shallow cave. Akela followed him. He sank down on to the edge of the pallet. Akela lay next to him, her warmth coming through his clothing. He drew his knees up and wrapped his arms about his legs. Gareth's head drooped onto his knees. He slept.

Gareth woke sometime in the night to feed the fire. This done he lay on his side curled up at the end of the pallet with Akela. His arm stretched out over her; her fur shielding his face. He slept again; deeper this time as only the young can sleep.

"NO! NO! Don't! NO!" Brant's moaning cries shattered Gareth's peaceful sleep. He woke with the instant fear and fight that comes with sudden alarm. His mind quickly brought him to himself and he turned to Brant.

"It's all right. It's all right. You're safe. It's all right." Words his mother and father had used when he had awakened crying in the night from childhood night terrors. "Shshshshsh, hush now." He said gently, softly.

His voice seemed to calm Brant and he eased back to into a quiet sleep. Gareth's heart was racing. He got up and put more wood on the fire. He squatted next to it letting its warmth calm him. The snow had gotten quite deep by now; several inches. He could see it in the firelight and the dull moonlight that filtered through the lowering clouds that shed the snow. He went back to his corner of the pallet, wrapped himself in his cloak and again with Akela next to him he slept.

Groaning woke him. Brant was moaning from his pain. Gareth knelt beside him with his cider in his hand. "Drink this." He pressed the jug to Brant's lips and held it there while Brant swallowed. "Can you eat? Are you hungry? I've got some bread and cheese here."

"What do you care?" snarled Brant.

"If I didn't care, I wouldn't be here. I wouldn't have come out searching for you."

"You just came out to bring me back to your father, Lord of the Manor, so he could punish me. Well, I've been punished haven't I? My own father saw to that!"

"Fine, stay hungry then! I'll eat it myself." And he put the bread to his lips.

"Wait" said Brant. "I'll eat it."

Gareth held the bread to Brant's mouth and Brant bit into it hungrily as if he were afraid Gareth would snatch the food away and mock him with it. He was still in pain and could hardly move. After he had eaten, Brant turned his back to Gareth and dozed again. Gareth got up and tended the fire. He really wasn't sure what else to do.

If a search party came then they wouldn't need more food, but what if no one came? What if they were here another day, another night? He stirred up the fire and started looking for more wood. It was harder to see now that snow covered everything, turning a familiar wood into a landscape of fantastical shapes and unrecognizable objects.

As he made his way through the wood he was thankful he'd worn his woolen socks his mother had knitted for him and the boots he used when he and his father hunted.

Gareth was nudging shapes in the snow with his foot to shake the snow from them looking for firewood already on the ground; anything to keep the fire going. He tapped a low mound and a rabbit shot out of it racing across the snow covered ground leaving a trail of footprints. Akela was on it in a moment, her long legs making up the distance. She had the rabbit in her mouth and was looking at Gareth as if to say. "Here's mine. Where's yours?" "Yes, where is mine?" Gareth said aloud.

He gathered up the wood and trekked back to the cave mouth. Brant was still sleeping. Gareth fed the fire and warmed his hands and feet. He knew someone would come, but when. How long would the two of them be here? Brant's arm was broken, that much was certain and he wasn't sure just what damage was done to his head when he hit the rocks and went into the water.

"Mother? Mother, are you there? I'm so cold, Mother." Brant's voice carried out of the cave. It had the strange unearthly sound of someone not in their right mind. Gareth rushed to him.

"Yes, I'm here, Brant. I'm right here."

Gareth spoke kindly to him trying to comfort him as his own mother had done, but in his heart he was terrified. What if Brant went crazy or died? He pulled up such cover as he had around Brant and sat with him until he fell into a fitful sleep.

"That settles that." Gareth said aloud to himself. "We need more food and warmth." To Akela he said, "Stay." Gareth gathered his bow and his quiver of arrows as Akela sat at the foot of the pallet with a slight whimper. She wanted to go with him. Gareth set off to where he had earlier seen deer tracks in the snow and began to follow them softly, soundlessly moving carefully through the wood taking care as he stepped to break no branch, make no noise. The wind was in his face as he tracked the deer. Then he saw more tracks, a herd. He could see large boulders ahead and recognized the place. There was a small dell below the rocks where the deer must be finding shelter from the wind.

He eased himself to the edge of the boulders and looked down into the snow covered glade. Here were a dozen deer, doe and yearlings.

Somewhere on watch would be the buck, but he wasn't interested in a trophy today only meat and a hide. Preferably attached to a doe he could manage to get back to the cave by himself. He chose the largest one and carefully nocked an arrow. He drew back his long bow the arrow's full length and let if fly. It struck the doe and she fell where she stood. The others instantly scattered in the gloom.

He went down and dressed her out there leaving the offal for the scavengers. He bound the legs together, slid a sapling he had hewed down through the legs and began the trek back to the camp. By the time he arrived the fire was down to embers and he himself was very cold. He got the fire going again, got the deer hung by her legs on a low branch and beginning skinning her out cutting around her feet and peeling off the hide.

He cut off one of the haunches and propped it over the fire to roast. He cut up the rest of the carcass and began the arduous task of putting it up high enough in a tree not to attract wolves.

He had moved some way from the camp. He kept coming back to check on Brant, feeding the fire and check on his roasting venison.

He washed the blood from his hands and drank water from the stream. By now Akela had left her post and was following him hoping to get her share of the deer. Gareth tossed her a piece of meat from time to time as he had worked. He laid the hide out on a rock and began to scrape it down. He washed it down in the stream and laid it by the fire to dry.

"I don't think we have time to tan this, do you Akela?" He said aloud to her. He cut another chunk of meat from the deer roast and popped it in his mouth. He would use the hide to cover Brant before nightfall. It was better than nothing. It had taken all day to hunt, dress the deer out and scrape the hide down. Night had fallen and still no sign of his father. Brant had continued to sleep. Gareth hoped he was recovering and not going deeper into a sleep from which he would not awaken. He made sure of Brant, drank some water and heaped more wood on the fire. Gareth was determined to stay up awhile and watch Brant.

The sky was still overcast and when the moon rose it gave a silver glow through the clouds to the heavens that filtered down to the snow covered wood. The stream was a dark rift in the whiteness.

Gareth was deep in his own thoughts when Brant spoke; not the strange frightening voice of his sleep, but a clear questioning sound.

"Why are you doing this? Why are you caring for me like a servant?" Gareth turned to see Brant sitting up on the pallet. His head still bandaged, but his eyes clear. "Why?"

"After you had beaten me and I was at home in my bed hurting, hardly able to move I thought that's how you must have felt . . . a lot. Everybody knows your father beats you and so I put myself in your place or rather", he said with a smile, "you had put me in your place. I don't know what I would have done growing up like you, but I didn't. My father loves me. He punishes me, but he never beats me. So I decided to find you and help you if I could."

"Why, why would you do that? I don't understand."

"Do you ever go to the chapel on Sundays when the priest gives a homily?"

"Not if I can help it!" Brant said with a bitter laugh. "Besides, I usually have to work in the scullery at the inn or serve if we have guests."

"Well, the priest, Father Kerry, was talking about Jesus and how He lived his life and what he taught. He said that Jesus said, 'Love your neighbor as you love yourself' and I got to thinking about that. Jesus served the disciples. He washed their feet."

"There'll be none of that!" Brant exclaimed.

"Well, no, but I washed your head, your wound and I fed you because you needed help. And I . . . forgive you for attacking me."

"I never asked you to forgive me."

"No, but I do nonetheless whether you want me too or not. I bear you no ill will. And I will stay here until we are found or until you can walk out of here yourself."

Brant was silent. Nothing in his life had prepared him for this. His mother loved him, he knew that, but she was too afraid of his father to protect him. He retreated into gruffness. "Give me some food." Gareth got up and cut some of the venison from the haunch roasting by the fire.

"Here is some water to wash it down.

We drank all the cider, I'm afraid." Brant took the meat in his hand. Gareth held the earthenware jug to Brant's lips as he drank deeply. Then he began to chew the meat. "More... please." Gareth cut another piece for him. "What's this covering me?"

"I shot a deer and skinned it. You needed to be warmer and we needed more food."

"Thank you." And with that Brant turned back over, wrapped himself in the deer hide and closed his eyes.

"Some watchman you are." Gareth's father's voice woke him with a start. Gareth jumped up and ran to him. "Father, I knew you would come."

"We came too" chimed Eamon and Aiden. Indeed as Gareth looked around it seemed that half the village was there by the stream.

"You seemed to have done all right for yourself." Smiled his father.

"Only because you taught me how, Father."

His father held him just a little tighter by the shoulders for a moment and then stepped back.

"I'm sorry we weren't sooner, but the snow made it hard to track you. I see you found Brant. " Brant had awakened when Eldred spoke and was sitting up with his head bowed. "Are you hurt?" Eldred asked.

"I was injured from the beating my father gave me, but I hurt my head when I tried again to attack your son. I'm very sorry. I know I have done wrong. I am ready to be punished."

"Well, we'll see about that later. Let's get you home and back to your mother."

"But what about my father? He will just beat me again."

"No, he will not. I have some news, for good or ill I cannot tell. Your father is dead. He fell into the kitchen fire while he was drunk and died. He will hurt no one anymore. I'm sorry that he is dead. I would not wish that on anyone, but I know he made life hard for you and your mother, but she needs you now to help run the inn. As to your crimes, you seem to have punished yourself quite enough. Can you walk?"

"Not well, but if we go slowly."

"I will help him, Father."

And so the procession wound its way slowly toward town; slogging through the heavy snow. They stopped at mid-day to make a fire and have a meal for which Eamon was thankful for the food and everyone else for the rest. Brant was quiet as Gareth served him the food the rescuers had brought with them. Gareth had stayed by Brant's side through the wood helping him over fallen timber, supporting him when he grew tired, asking his father to stop once more for Brant to rest.

Finally they made their way back to the village and Brant's home where he was welcomed with hugs and tears from his mother. "I will come tomorrow to see how you are faring." Gareth said.

"Thank you; we would welcome your visit." Brant's mother replied. Brant nodded once in silent agreement. As they reached the village the entourage had dispersed with each one going his own way until it was just Gareth and his father together on the last leg to the manor house; Akela by their side. "I see you decided what to do about Brant," said his father. "You have chosen wisely. To be a good leader, one must be willing to serve."

THE END

3

THE SPIRIT OF FEAR

Matthias crouched silently, his knobby knees poking through his coarse woven breeches. His cloak wrapped around him, his hood pulled over his head to ward off the damp as the sun set. He knew the deer came this way and he was determined to get one, his first. He had successfully eluded his tutor, his father, his mother and most importantly his older brother, Niles. His yew bow was ready with an arrow handy to be nocked and released should some hapless deer wander by.

It was early evening just at dusk when the deer began to move to feed before they would bed for the night. He was in the hedgerow by his father's barley fields waiting for the deer to come to the grain to forage for the night. The gloom darkened and the cold set in. He began to wonder just how long he would have to stay here before he could claim his quarry. A stag would be nice, something big, with giant antlers. That would show his brother! But even a doe would be good. He envisioned his triumph.

Shooting the deer: dressing it out just as he had seen his father do: dragging it home: the mighty hunter, the look of pride on his father's face; his brother's shock at being bested. These thoughts were beginning to warm him in the darkening air. Night had fallen. The moon was not yet up and Matthias wasn't sure he could see a deer to shoot it unless it stumbled across him. Yes, that would be even better. He would pull out his knife and kill the deer with his bare hands! He shifted just a little to ease his burning haunches trying to be as quiet as he could.

When is the blasted deer going to come he thought to himself? Then he heard it. Movement. Something big, something heavy coming his way. This must be the biggest stag in the country: in the world!

His heart raced as he slowly brought the arrow to the bow and carefully eased the nock to the string. He wouldn't pull back yet. We could just barely pull the bow and he wasn't sure how long he could hold the arrow fully drawn. Suddenly he heard a noise like thunder and a stream of fire lit the night. Dragons! A dragon had come.

He was the hunted, not the hunter. In a moment he jumped up, running as fast as his thin legs could go through the hedge, across the fields toward the lodge away from the dragon. Was it drawing closer? Could it fly as the tales had said? Could they defeat it? Would it eat them all and live in their great house laying waste to the land?   He was running, running, running, flying across the fields; his quiver beating time on his back driving him with every step; urging him onward. He could see the village now. The smoke from the peat fires hanging on the night air.

He could see small squares of light filtering through the hides stretched across the windows. Should he cry out? Should he warn the village? He tried to shout, but his breath would not come.

He was running and he was afraid to stop lest the dragon should catch him and then it would be too late. There! There was the great door. There was home! He grabbed the latch and swung the heavy oaken door on its iron hinges. His father was in the great hall talking to someone. There were others, strangers. His mother was seated by the fire. Didn't they realize there was a dragon? Was he the first to bring the news?

He stopped his chest heaving, his legs felt like water. In a moment he got his breath. "Dragons! Dragons! The dragon is here!" He shouted at the top of his lungs. All eyes turned to him in an instant. His father had the dark look of one who has been interrupted and his mother dropped her needlepoint. The strangers continued to stare. "I was hunting deer . . . the edge of the field . . . dragon . . . attack me. . . Right behind me. I heard him. I saw him breathe fire!" All this tumbled out in a rush as Matthias tried to get his breath.

Suddenly his father, Martin, let out a great bellowing laugh. "You saw a dragon, Matthias? And he chased you?" "Yes, Father! He chased me through the fields. He's coming. We must get ready to kill him."

"Well, St. George, how should we kill this dragon? Boar spears? Poison tipped arrows?" "I don't know Father! You must kill it."

In that moment those in the great hall began to recover from the interruption. Some smiled, some laughed openly. Did they not believe him? Did they not understand the danger? Why were they smiling? "You've got to believe me!" His mother rose from her seat and came to him. She put her arm around him. He shrugged it off. "What did you see, my son?" "I saw fire. I heard the dragon roar!"

At that moment, Niles burst in the room laughing with a young stranger just behind him. "Here is your dragon!" At that moment the stranger put a fire brand to his lips and blew fire.

Niles took a flat drum and drew his resin tipped finger across it making it roar. "You should have seen your face. I've never seen you run so fast!

Frightened rabbits have nothing on you. You should be a royal messenger with your speed. Here is your bow. You dropped it as you ran." The hall burst into laughter as this.

Tears burst from Matthias and he fled from the room. Anger, frustration, hurt welled up within him, filled him. He ran through the hall toward his rooms and fell into his bed. Hot tears soaked his pillow as his body heaved with sob after sob. He heard the hinges on his door squeak as they always did when he tried to open it slowly. "Go away, Mother! I don't want to see you." "It's not your mother, Matthias," his father said in a low voice.

He came silently across the room and sat on Matthias' bed. He put his large heavy hand on Matthias' back. Matthias could feel the warmth of it through the fabric of his clothes. "Niles' trick was very cruel and I'm sorry I laughed, but I thought it was some jest you were having on us all. I thought you were playing. Please, forgive me. When I realized that the joke had been played on you to embarrass you, I spoke sharply to Niles and his young fire-breathing friend.

He is one of the troupe who has come to entertain us for a while. It was his master to whom I was speaking when you burst in with your tale. Matthias turned slowly, sat up and pulled his knees to his chest.

His father's arms enveloped him and Matthias allowed himself to be engulfed in his father's embrace. He could feel the strength that coursed through his father's limbs.

"I ran, Father. I was scared. I am a coward." "No, you ran to warn us. Besides, if there were a dragon what were you going to do against him? Worry him to death like you do your mother and your tutor? There are things to fear, things worthy of fear.

It's what you do with the fear that determines whether you are courageous or a coward. Running to warn us was a brave and honorable thing to do. You could have run anywhere, but you ran here. You ran home to those you love and who love you. In the midst of your fear you kept your head. Do you remember Father Alenot's homily on I Timotheus? 'God has not given us the spirit of fear, but of power and of love and of a sound mind?'

Or the words of Jesus in the book of John "*pacem relinquo vobis pacem meam do vobis non quomodo mundus dat ego do vobis non turbetur cor vestrum neque formidet*" 'Peace I leave with you, my peace I give unto you: not as the world giveth, give I unto you. Let not your heart be troubled, neither let it be afraid.' Now, do you really believe there are dragons?"

"No," Matthias whispered through the folds of his father's tunic. "You know there is no such thing, but in the moment you let your fear override your reason. Now, I have spoken to Niles and no doubt he's not really ashamed of what he did, but you need to forgive him. It isn't easy being the younger brother. Dry your eye, swallow your pride and come to supper. The troupe will perform and entertain us. There are minstrels, jugglers and you've already met the fire breather. Come when you are ready." His father stood, ruffled Matthias' hair and silently left the room.

Matthias got up. He splashed water on his face from the ewer that sat on the table in his room. He dried his face and his eyes. He straightened his tunic and tried to make himself look presentable. He made his way to the great hall where the evening meal was being served.

He silently went to his place at the table unnoticed. Everyone was watching the juggler performing in the middle of the room.

He started with two brightly colored leather spheres juggled with one hand then he added another ball, three with two hands, then another, four balls, then another, five balls, then another, six. His hands were a whirr and the brightly colored spheres seemed like a circular blur floating in mid-air. He changed the pace and the balls went higher and higher reaching to the darkness near the top of the thatched ceiling far from the candlelight. A jester came after him trying to mimic his skill. Everyone laughed when the balls came crashing down on his head. He caught one on the back of his neck, flipped it up and caught it on his forehead.

With a quick flick of his neck he sent the ball flying high. He pretended to look for it as it landed on his hat and made the bells attached to the ends of it jingle. He proceeded around the room looking for the ball disrupting people at their seats, making antic faces and remarks about the guests that made everyone laugh.

He ended his jests by tipping Nile's chair over tumbling him to the floor. Niles sprang up with anger in his eyes, but knew better than to lose his temper in front of all the guests.

The jester made a fumbling apology that also brought peals of laughter from the people by its delivery and left as the minstrel came to the center of the room with his lute and began to sing. He had a beautiful clear voice that wrapped itself around every note. He sang a ballad about St. George and the dragon that made Matthias turn red in the face, but he soon realized it was not directed at himself but simply part of the flow of songs. The minstrel was joined by a red haired girl a couple of years older than Matthias. Her skin was like cream and her voice Matthias thought was how angels must sound.

He was smitten but as he looked around the room to see if anyone noticed he saw that he was not the only one. Niles was staring with an open mouth and the glazed look of one who has lost his senses. The two continued their program singing sometimes as a duet, sometimes as a solo each performing in their turn.

At the end of the concert the minstrel bowed and the girl gave a low curtsey, went to Matthias's mother and gave her a small bouquet of flowers. The house broke into loud applause as two acrobats entered tumbling around the room seeming to float like magic through the air. Matthias continued to eat, hoping his own interlude of the afternoon was forgotten, but he could see by looks stolen in sidelong glances and the smiles that followed that it wasn't completely gone from peoples' minds.

Finally the entertainment drew to a close. People from the village invited to join the evening's entertainment made their way home. His father's household began to clean up after the meal and Matthias himself grew tired. He went to his mother and father and bade them good night. He nodded at Niles who smirked and nodded back at him. He mouthed the words, "good night, rabbit" as Matthias passed by him. Again Matthias' face burned with the memory.

After breaking his fast the next morning Matthias was with his tutor for his lessons. After that he went to Father Alenot for Latin and French.

Sometimes Matthias wished his father wasn't quite so concerned about his son's education, but Matthias did enjoy learning and Father Alenot would usually tell him stories about his travels after the lessons were completed. Father Alenot had been to the Holy Land.

He had been to Italy. He had even traveled to North Africa across the Mediterranean Sea. When Matthias' lessons and chores were done for the day he sought out the troupe of performers. They were camped out in one of his father's tithe barns.

The troupe had made themselves comfortable in the way people used to the traveling life do where ever they are. He wanted to find the jester, but he also hoped to catch a glimpse of the red haired girl. Matthias had learned the jester's name was Guignot. He saw him stripped to the waist chopping wood. He looked completely different that he had with his jester's had and bells and his floppy clothes from the night before.

This was a serious young man who looked like he was cleaving dragons with every swing of the axe. "Master Guignot" Matthias spoke hesitantly.

The jester stopped mid-swing, put down the axe and turned, a smile curled on his lips. "Just Guignot, young master, I'm not grand enough to have Master in front of my name. At your service." "Sorry, Ma. . . . Guignot, I'm Matthias." "I know who you are. I saw you storm into the great room yesterday shouting about dragons." Matthias' face reddened again. He looked down, embarrassed. "That was a cruel trick your brother pulled on you, and I cuffed Anselm on the ear for his part in it. I make people laugh but never at someone else's expense. Bully's do that." "You tipped my brother's chair over on purpose last night." "Young master, would I do such a thing as that? It was all part of the act." Matthias found his courage after that and asked, "Guignot, would you teach me to catch a ball on the back of my neck and on my forehead?" "What's in it for me, young master?"

Matthias could see he didn't really mean this, but he answered, "I'll chop your wood for you." "Fair enough, there are only a few more pieces to split. Here," he handed the axe to Matthias and stood back to watch Matthias struggle with the weight.

Matthias spit on his hands as he had seen his father's woodsman do before starting to split the wood for the household and began to swing the axe. He caught the edge of the log and sent it flying. "Here," said Guignot. "None of that now. Grip the axe here. Keep your eyes on the log, they are devious and will jump at you if you don't fix your eye on them. Swing the axe to its full length and just before you hit the log give a snap to your wrists." Matthias followed these directions and was rewarded when the log went flying split cleanly in the middle. The others went the same way and Matthias felt satisfyingly accomplished as he leaned the axe against the pile of wood.

"Well done, Master Matthias. Well done." Guignot had put on his shirt and jerkin. He rummaged in his bag and brought out the colored leather balls he had used the night before. "Here." He handed them to Matthias. They were filled with sand. He could hear it as he kneaded them between his fingers.

It was a soft scrunching sound. He tossed them lightly in his hand to feel their weight. "The secret to these is they don't bounce. The sand makes them stay where they land. Watch."

Guignot tossed the balls in the air and let them fall. Each stayed where it landed. Then he tossed them again and caught them on the back of his neck. "You have to have a sense of where the ball is in the air and where you are. Do you understand? Close your eyes."

Matthias closed his eyes. "Stretch out your arms." Matthias stretched out his arms. "Now, with your eyes closed and your arms stretched out, touch your nose." Matthias frowned then smiled at the thought of how he must look and brought his finger unerringly right to his nose. "Very good! Again with each hand now." Matthias could touch his nose with both hands without any hesitation. "Now, take a ball. Toss it and catch it with your eyes closed. Not too high now to start." Matthias obediently tossed the ball and caught it.

He tossed it a bit higher and caught it again. Higher still and he caught it. He had a sense of where the ball was and where his hand was together. Then he tried it a little higher and heard the thump of the ball as it hit the ground. "So you're not perfect, who is? You toss the ball to me, nice and slow, underhanded like this." He made a motion with his arm.

Matthias brought his arm back and made the toss. Guignot watch the ball rise, shifted his feet a little and at the last moment ducked his head and caught the ball neatly on the back of his neck. "Good toss! Again." Again Matthias made the toss, again Guignot caught the ball on his neck. "Now, your turn." Guignot tossed the ball. Matthias watched it, ducked his head too soon and felt the ball strike him in the back of the neck and roll off. "Again." This time Matthias waited a little longer to duck his head. The ball landed between his shoulders. He stayed there bent over flapping his arms to keep his balance and try to toss the ball from the middle of his back. "You look like a goose flapping like that. Here." They both laughed as Guignot took the ball from Matthias' back and they tried again.

Again and again they practiced and slowly Matthias began to get the feel for the trick until he could catch the ball on his neck every time. "We should stop for now. Have you learned what you wanted to learn?"

"Yes, thank you." "Is there anything else?" "Well, if you could tell me the name of the singer, I would like that." "Malcolm, his name is Malcolm. He's the leader of our troupe."

"That's not who I mean." "Oh, the girl, you want the girl's name. Sorry, it is Angharad." "Thanks." Guignot watched the boy skip back to the house. "Not quite a boy, not yet a man. He will find his way."

Matthias smiled as he went back into the manor. He thought it would be good if he cleaned up a bit before the evening meal. Angharad might be singing again. Matthias began whistling as he made his toilet and prepared for dinner. He chose his best tunic. He even tried to run the bone comb through his hair but it didn't seem to help. He made his way in some state to the table and sat quietly waiting for the meal to begin. His father and mother came to the head of the table. Again there were at table some of the wealthier villagers, the gold smith, the wine merchant. Father Alenot was seated beside Matthias.

Niles sat in his usual place, but Matthias noticed he was in his best tunic as well and some scent wafted around Niles that Matthias had never smelled before, much nicer than the older brother smell that usually accompanied Niles.

The meal began with thanks to God and after the first course the performers began again. The tumblers were first this time accomplishing more death defying acrobatics.

Then came the juggler and the fire-breathing young man who had added setting something alight on his hand that made his fingers appear to be on fire. Then the minstrel and Angharad. Tonight the songs were more comic and light-hearted. As they sang Guignot pranced around in time with the music and added his own comic words to the tunes. While the singing continued Guignot began his juggling and catching the ball on his neck and forehead.

He dragged Niles onto the floor and showed him what to do. At first Niles resisted not wishing to be made fool of, but he saw a smile on Angharad's lips and thought to cover himself with praise. It was not to be.

With every toss of the leather balls Niles failed to catch them and Guignot made such fun of him the hall was laughing at Niles, not with him. In bad grace he stalked off to take his seat. Then Guignot motioned to Matthias. Nervously Matthias moved to the center of the U-shape made by the surrounding tables.

Through all this the singing continued. By now everyone was expecting the same show Niles had made, but with the first throw of the brightly colored balls by Guignot Matthias caught it squarely on the back of his neck and tossed it expertly up to catch in again on his forehead. Then he began to toss the balls to Guignot who sent them flying back to be caught again and so the flow went back and forth until the hall was applauding.

Guignot caught the last toss and took Matthias by the hand and they bowed together. Matthias saw that Niles was in a mood, but Angharad was smiling. The evening ended. On their way down the hall to their rooms Niles gave Matthias a shove that sent him reeling into the wall.

A scuffle ensued that ended with Father pulling Niles off Matthias and shaking them both soundly. "Go to your rooms. Such behavior is not in keeping with a drunken brawl at a public house much less in our manor. Mind your clothes. To bed with you both!"

The next morning both the boys were sullen at breakfast. "After your lessons I want you both to clean the stables." "Father, we have stable hands for that." Niles said. "Yes, and since you've been acting like a pair of stable hands you can do their work! I've told them to expect you." "But I have. . . I was going to meet. . ." "Yes!?" Father exclaimed. "I was going to take Angharad walking in the woods, perhaps hunt a little." "I see. And what does Angharad's father say to this plan?" "Her father?" "Yes, the minstrel is her father and he might object to his only daughter walking in the woods with a young man." "It's only a walk." Niles grumbled. "Nevertheless, you should ask his permission before you walk with his daughter in the wood. . . AFTER you clean the stables."

The day passed slowly with the knowledge of the coming unpleasant task waiting both the boys. They had put on their roughest clothes and went sullenly and silently to the barn. The grooms greeted them with suppressed smiles as they handed them the wooden scoops and rakes with which to clean the stable then they made themselves scarce. It was one thing to laugh at another's misfortune; it was another to watch it.

The boys began grudgingly but it wasn't long before Matthias began to accept the task while not with joy at least absorption. He liked the smell of the hay and the feed. There was a companionable element to leading each horse out while he cleaned the stall; leading them back in again and patting them on the neck. They had decided to each take a side and while Matthias was steadily completing his task, Niles grumbled and complained with every pull of the rake, every push of the scoop. "Why today of all days? Why do I have to do groom's work? One day I will be Lord of the Manor. I will never order my son's to do groom's work." And so it went until Niles voice was a murmur in the background ignored by Matthias. Lead each horse out; talk to them gently, clean their stall and move on.

He had procured a few precious carrots from cook for his favorites and these he fed secretly lest the other horses find out. Just as he finished the last stall, Angharad arrived at the stable. Niles came out of another stall threw down his rake and went to her. "You finish this. I'm going. Come, Angharad." "You're just going to leave your brother to do your work?" "Yes. He won't mind. He's just a child."

"Well, my father says I can go with you, but perhaps you'd like to clean up a bit first? You smell of horses and not in a good way." "I'll be right back." With that Niles rushed off to the manor leaving Angharad standing in the middle of the stable. Matthias looked down, picked up the rake his brother had left lying tines up before anyone could step on it and get hit in the face. "You don't mind that he treats you like that?" "Not really. It's a job like any other." "You did well last night with the juggling. Guignot told me he had worked with you. That you wanted to learn the trick." "Thank you. Why are you going with my brother?" "Well, I like walking in the wood and I don't like going alone.

It's not always safe so if I had the choice of not walking or walking with your brother, I choose to walk, but walking is all I'm doing, your brother just happens to be along." Niles arrived at that moment reeking of the scent he had worn last night. "For certain did you fall into a vat of scented oil, Niles?" "What do you mean?"

"Well, it's better than the other smell, but we won't be sneaking up on any deer with oil of clove going before us. Come on."

The two of them left. Matthias smiled as he saw Niles grab for Angharad's hand and she shook him off. Matthias finished the stalls in silence and went back to the house to clean up. While he was washing the stable off his skin he decided to track Niles and Angharad. Perhaps he could frighten Niles as Niles had frightened him. He took the long dagger his grandfather had given him. It was Viking made and had a horse's head at the top of the hilt. The handle was made from a deer antler.

It was large in his hands, but he would grow into it his grandfather had said. He tied the sheath to his leather belt. He slung his quiver over his shoulder and took his bow.

He wasn't planning on using it, but he felt better with it in his hand. His father saw him in the hall on his way out. "Did you finish the stables?" "Yes, Father. They are completely clean with new straw. The stable boys were laughing at us." "You don't begrudge them a laugh at your expense do you?" "I suppose not, as long as I don't have to do it every day." "Then no more fighting in the hall with your brother, yes?" "Yes, Father." "Go on with you now, good hunting."

Matthias smiled as he swung the great door open and closed again. Yes, good hunting, but you don't know what I'm hunting, he thought to himself. He stopped for a moment considering which way Niles went. There were the dales to the south of the Manor House and the forest to the east, but the stream that flowed across his father's estates had a good path and was a pleasant walk. He eased along the path beside the stream trying to be as silent as he could his soft leather boots making little sound in the yielding grass. How far had they gotten he wondered. There was a pool higher up the stream surrounded by large boulders. Perhaps they went there to sit on the rocks. Not far from there was a meadow filled with flowers. That would be a good choice for his lady love. There was an enormous oak in the middle of the glen to sit under and enjoy the beauty of the glade.

He would follow the stream that far and then make for the glade. He went slowly lest he should come up on them before he knew it and they would hear him. He moved silently as if he were hunting deer. Silence took time his father had told him.

He had been moving for some time when he reached the edges of the pool. It was deep but clear and he could see the large trout moving in the depths where the channel of the stream brought the food to them. On another day he might come back to test his wits against the fish, but today he had something else on his mind. He did stop to think about testing his arrows against the fish, but he knew you had to shoot where the fish weren't and he couldn't quite work that out right now. He had seen his father's huntsman stand completely frozen and release an arrow with a barb and a line to draw the fish from the water and actually do it but that was beyond his skill right now. Someday, perhaps.

Matthias eased his head slowly above a boulder to see if the couple were there and then decide how best to frighten them, but the rocks around the pool held only silence. He knew roughly the way to the meadow, but he wanted to make certain he was not seen or heard. He began picking his way through the bracken yards off the path so that he could see without being seen.

This walk was not going as Niles had expected. He had had visions of walking through the forest hand in hand with Angharad, perhaps lying on the rocks by the pool with his head in her lap as she ran her fingers through his hair.

First she told him he smelled, then she said he had too much scent of clove. There was to be no hand holding and it was all too clear to him that no fingers belonging to Angharad would be running through his hair. More like a finger in his eye. With every step he grew more sullen and the more sullen he became the more she laughed at him and mocked him. Then she began to berate him for the way he treated his brother, leaving him with all the work to do and skiving off with her. Matthias was a kid, a blot, what did he matter? She went on and on about it.

Then she talked about Matthias skill catching the balls on his neck like the jester as if that were something! What about him? He was quite tall for his age and strong. Some girls in the village thought him handsome. True there weren't many his age in the village and those girls had never been out of the village, but still. On they walked Angharad trilling on and Niles sullenly silent.

They reached the pool which had so recently featured in his visions. "Here is our trout pool. We come here sometimes to fish." "It's lovely. It's like its own little world."Angharad exclaimed. "The way the trees overhang the brook and the rocks surround the pool. Very lovely." "Not as lovely as you, Angharad." Niles said boldly, but woodenly. He had heard his father say this to his mother and gagged at the time, but this was perhaps the way to talk to a girl. "What a silly thing to say, Niles. Did you hear that somewhere?" Niles' face reddened but he plowed on oblivious to the danger he was getting into. "Would you like to sit by the water on one of the rocks. It's nice here. You said so yourself."

"We can sit for a bit to rest, Niles, but don't get any ideas. It's not like I'm going to let you put your head in my lap and run my fingers through your hair. What an idea? I'd probably get bitten by something living in your hair?" Could she read his mind? What is it with girls? And he didn't have lice. He bathed once a week whether he needed to or not, his mother made him and he washed his face and hands every day.

They sat by the pool for a while to enjoy the cool and the sound of the stream. Niles tried to think of something to say that she wouldn't mock or hurl back in his face. Fishing. That was it. He was good at fishing. "I caught a big trout here not long ago." "Did you, now?" Was there mocking in her voice? He couldn't tell. "Yes, I caught a big trout here and cleaned it myself. First I bashed it in the head with a rock to keep it from flopping around and then I gutted it with my knife right there where you are sitting. Guts everywhere. You could see what it had been eating. And the smell. Phew! The crow came and started eating the innards while we watched. But the trout tasted great when we got it home."

"Niles, you really know how to win a girls heart. Let's go." Angharad got up quickly brushing at her dress as if the fish guts might be clinging to it. So Niles thought she likes to hear me talk about fishing and hunting and how good I am at it. He would take her to the meadow and show her where he got his first deer and hung it up on the great oak to dress it. She must really want to see the place because she is walking lots faster now. Great!

Niles began to tell her about all the rabbits he had gotten last winter. How he hit them in the head with a club when he found them live in his snares, even the young ones. He went on to tell her about the fox he killed and how he had cleaned it and scraped out it's hide leaving the head on so his mother could have a fur for her hood. Now they were going much faster. Angharad really could walk. She was a good walker. He was struggling to keep up with her even with his long stride and she wasn't saying anything now about his brother or the way he smelled. He was finally impressing her. Before he knew it they were at the meadow with the great oak tree. "Here we are." Niles said.

"Really, I never would have known this was the meadow with the great oak tree you've been taking about for the last eon just because it's a meadow with a great oak tree in the middle. Are you certain this is the only one?" "Oh yes. It's the one." Niles answered. Was Angharad not listening to him? Maybe she wasn't as smart as he thought. The idea that she was mocking him somehow never entered his mind.

Finally she was slowing down. They walked slowly to the tree to get into its shade. There was no place to sit except the ground and so they sat with their backs against the tree. "I brought an apple with me, would you like some? I didn't think you would think about bringing anything to eat." "Yes, thank you." Niles said. This was even better. She was feeding him. "Would you like me to cut the apple for you? I have my knife." "Is that the knife you used to gut the trout?" Niles looked at it for a moment. "I think so." "No thank you. I've got a knife."

Angharad took a small silver knife from her bag. It was sheathed in dark purple and had a small jewel in the handle, but it was very sharp. She pared the apple quickly and cut it in pieces for them.

She laid it out on an embroidered handkerchief between them. Niles began to talk about the deer he shot but Angharad forestalled him. "I'm going to rest my eyes for a bit. Could you be quiet, please?" It was the only thing she could think of to keep him quiet. She leaned back against the tree and shifted a bit to make herself more comfortable. Her eyes were closed.

Niles just sat like a stone but then he too began to feel sleepy. He closed his eyes imagining Angharad waking him with a kiss. All was quiet in the glade.

A howl woke both of them. Then another howl. Niles jumped up and began to look around. Angharad was already awake and circling the tree to see the source of the howling. Wolves, a pack of them on the edge of the meadow. More were gathering, Angharad counted six, maybe seven. She couldn't see them clearly in the edges of the glade. Niles saw the danger and started to run.

"We will never out run them." Niles had been thinking only of himself for the moment, but not even he would leave a girl helpless in the forest surrounded by wolves. He was in a panic. They couldn't run and there was no place to hide. "The tree," Angharad shouted. "We've got to get in the tree." "The limbs are too high." Niles squeaked. His voice rising with the fear. "You boost me up and I'll pull you up after me." "Yes, yes!"

Angharad quickly gathered up her things, wiping her knife on her handkerchief and putting it back in its sheath. She turned to face the tree and lifted her foot for Niles to take. He hesitated. "Take my foot you idiot and help me in the tree or we will both be dead. Now!" Niles snapped into the present took her small foot in his hands and lifted her up. There was a flash of shift and she was in the tree with her hand stretched out to him. "Come on! Hurry!" She shouted. Niles froze. He turned and saw the wolves coming toward them. Flanking, swerving hemming them in. Even if he was able to move his feet and legs there was no place to run. He screamed and screamed. Angharad was shouting at him. "Take my hand. I can pull you up. Hurry before it's too late!" The wolves were on them. The big male hanging back, the younger males dashing forward pulling back, growling, snapping, howling. The first one lunged at Niles as he cowered against the tree.

There was a silver flash and the wolf began to yipe, turning to bite at the knife embedded in its flank. Angharad had thrown her beautiful silver knife.

Slowly Niles drew his blade, but his hands were shaking so badly he had to use both to hold it. He began to yell and wave it about him. Sweat had broken out on his forehead and tears were streaming from his eyes. At that moment one of the wolves fell dead with an arrow in its side.

Matthias was moving slowly through the woods along the path he knew they must follow. Then he saw it, the paw print, a wolf print exactly like the one the huntsman had shown him one day when they were out shooting arrows in the wood. His words came back to Matthias. "If you see one print look for more. Wolves travel in packs." And there they were. Many prints. Matthias couldn't tell how many, but there were a lot of them. All thought of sneaking and frightening left him in the reality of true fear. Wolves could kill. He had seen what a pack had done to his father's flock of sheep. He looked around trying to see through the trees. Looking for dark shapes low to the ground. Nothing. He knew he couldn't be too far from the clearing. If only Niles and Angharad were there. He could find them. They would be safe. Then he heard the howling. His heart began to race and his mouth went dry.

Matthias started to run through the woods in the direction of the meadow. He dodged this way and that around the trees as he ran. The howling was growing louder and more frequent. He broke through the tree line to see Niles alone surrounded by the wolf pack. A moment of thought questioned why was Niles alone but in the moment it was gone. He heard Niles screaming and crying. He heard the wolves howling as he ran. There was a yelp from one young wolf and he could see it circling itself biting at its rump. Without a thought Matthias reached over his shoulder for his arrows.

As swift as a thought he let fly toward a wolf. His arrow found its mark. Then another and another as the wolves began to fall under his bow. Niles saw the wolf fall and then two others. His mind could not grasp what was happening. Had his father found them? Could it be the huntsman?

Another wolf fell. Niles could see a figure, but because of the tears did not know who it was. Another wolf fell. Angharad continued to shout at him and hold out her hand but he was turned away from her.

Another wolf fell sprouting an arrow from his side, blood staining the grass red. Matthias was stalking nearer now wary lest there should be others of the pack holding back from the attack hidden in the woods. He released another arrow. Another wolf fell. He edged closer. He saw a white hand and arm coming from the tree and knew Angharad was there. In his mind it registered that Niles must have helped her, but why hadn't he come up after her. He was closer now and he had killed another of the wolves surrounding the tree. There was only one left but he could not shoot it for fear of hitting Niles.

Niles was out of his mind with fear. Wolves were falling, bleeding all around him. He was paralyzed. He could not move. Could not think. He slowly began to sink to his knees and wrap his arms around himself. The big male edged closer, his yellow eyes fixed on Niles. Niles was curled into a ball now all thought ceased.

Matthias saw all this and ran to his brother. As he ran he dropped his bow and pulled out his grandfather's dagger.

With no other thought except to save Niles, Matthias launched himself through the air crashing into the big wolf. The wolf turned snarling as Matthias dagger sank into his heart. Blood spurted out blinding Matthias as the two bodies collapsed together.

A soft hand touched his shoulder and a soft voice called his name. "Matthias, Matthias, are you all right?" Matthias blinked and rolled off the smelly wolf. The wet stickiness of blood filling his nose and coating his skin. He looked up to see Angharad kneeling beside him wiping his face with her handkerchief. "Niles?" "He's all right. He's only fainted. That was the bravest and most stupid thing I've ever seen. You could have been killed. Weren't you afraid, boy?"

"My father said 'everyone has fear. It's what you do with it that matters.'" Matthias tried to get up but his legs wouldn't move. He rolled over on his knees and with Angharad's help he stood. He went slowly over to Niles and shook him.

Niles eyes opened and he saw Matthias. Shame came into his eyes as he remembered what had happened. "I am a coward." It was as if they had changed places.

"I was so proud. I was thinking only about myself."

"No, next time you'll know what to do. Next time you won't be frozen." Mathias said.

"I was filled with pride trying to impress Angharad. I was thinking only about myself." At that moment there was a shout from across the meadow. The three of them turned expecting another attack.

What they saw were archers emerging from the wood's edge. "It's Father!" Matthias exclaimed. Martin, the Huntsman and several of his father's men came out of the edge of the forest. They were armed, with arrows nocked and bows drawn. The three young people stood silently, somewhat sheepishly as the men approached.

"What has happened here?" Father asked.

"Wolves, Father," Niles quavered. "Wolves attacked Angharad and I as we sat by the tree, but Matthias saved us. He shot the wolves with his bow and the big one he killed with his dagger as it attacked me. He saved our lives, Father."

"It was attacking Niles." Matthias said simply as if that explained everything. "It was trying to eat him."

His father smiled a grim smile as he looked around. "This looks like a battle field. The Huntsman saw the wolf signs and heard their howling. He knew you were in the woods and raced to get help. We followed the path and figured you'd come here."

"No use wasting good wolf pelts" said the Huntsman and with that he began to dress them out. The other men just looked at the three young people; Niles with his tear stained face, Angharad as cool as could be, her red hair glowing in the sunset and Matthias who looked like a fiend with his face and clothes covered in blood and his matted hair standing on end.

"Come," Father said. "Let's go home. They will deal with this."

With the Huntsman finishing his grim task and the other men staying to help him the four began their weary way back to the Manor house.

Along the way, Niles, Angharad and Matthias told their story; each speaking over the other with some forgotten detail or thought. Matthias was a little shame-faced about his plan to scare Niles but no one seemed to mind too much. They reached the Manor house and the boys' mother threw her arms around them, holding them to her without a single word about how they looked or smelled. After a while she said, "Go, wash now. We will eat soon and guests are coming to hear the entertainment." Soon the boys were splashing water on each other as the fear and danger washed off them with the dirt and blood.

"Thank you for being brave." Niles said to Matthias. "I'm sorry I tried to frighten you with the dragon."

"It's all right. I was going to frighten you."

"Yes, but I don't suppose you gathered the wolves together just for that."

"No. I never thought of that." The brothers finished their ablutions, dressed and walked in friendship together into the great hall.

By now the reports of their exploits had traveled around the village and were known to everyone. "Let us give thanks." Father said. "Dearest Lord, we thank Thee for the protection and deliverance You have given this day. We thank Thee for lessons learned and lives saved. We thank Thee loving Father for the great salvation You offer us through Your Son, Jesus Christ. I thank Thee for the lives of my sons and for the life of Angharad. Amen." And the hall answered together, "Amen" with the voice of Angharad's father echoing the sound.

The meal began in earnest with Father Alenot questioning Matthias closely about his exploits thinking privately to use them in his homily the next Sabbath day. The entertainments began again with the jugglers and acrobats diverting the crowd's attention from Matthias for which he was thankful. He hadn't set out to rescue his brother and Angharad, it just happened. "Everyone has fear," his father's words echoed in his head, "It's what you do with it than matters." The meal was winding to a close with the sweet things being served out when Angharad and her father stepped into the center of the hall for their performance.

Angharad looked like a princess there in the midst of the crowd. Her father began to strum his lute and Angharad pulled a parchment from her sleeve and held it so the two singers could see the words together. They began to sing in their high clear voices. "The wild wolves were wandering across the dark way. . . ."

The song told the tale of all that had happened making the walk more romantic for poetry sake than it really was and giving Niles some credit for getting Angharad to safety in the "mighty oaken tree" but "Matthias Wolf-bane" featured heavily in the song about his bravery, his "stout heart and steady hand" the "flight of his arrow true and finishing with "struck with his bold Viking blade."

When the ballad was finished the hall erupted in applause and the minstrels had to sing the song through three more times before the guests were satisfied and by the third time the people in the hall were echoing the words, "struck with his bold Viking blade." Matthias's face was as red as Angharad's hair, but his father and mother were bursting with pride because of their son.

The troupe stayed on Lord Martin's lands for some time taking a rest and honing their skills. With winter coming on it was a safe warm place to be in those turbulent times. The three young people became inseparable like brothers and sister strolling through the forests, hunting, fishing and spending time together.

Guignot taught Matthias more tricks and even Niles learned some of the tumbling stunts of the acrobats. Malcolm gave the boys lessons in music at their mother's behest and Matthias became quite proficient on the lute, although he vowed he would never sing the song about Matthias Wolf-bane. Lady Eryn, Matthias's mother, had each of them cloaks made trimmed in wolf fur to see them through the winter. That spring when the fairs began to call to the troupe of performers Malcolm, Angharad and Guignot bade them farewell vowing to see them again in the fall when the season of travel was over.

The years passed and the tanned wolf hides on the wall of the Manor house grew dusty with age and time rolled on as time does, but throughout their lives the words from First Timotheus lived in the hearts of the two brothers, "God has not given us a spirit of fear, but of power and love and of a sound mind."

The End.

4

FOLLOW THE KING

In October 937 AD there was a great battle that united England under King Athelstan who history tells us was a pious and learned king. He was the grandson of Alfred the Great. No one knows the exact location, but history describes this battle with these words, **'Never yet within this island has there been a greater slaughter of folk felled by sword's edges'**. This is the story of a young man who chose to follow the King.

The shock of the blow ran through Edric's arm and shoulder like lightening. He had never felt such a jolt before. He nearly dropped his sword.

He stepped back with a look of hurt and surprise on his face as Alaric pressed his advantage and knocked him down with a lowered shoulder.

"Never hesitate! If I'd been a Pict or a Norseman you'd be dead with your head on the ground. What did you think fighting was going to be like, picking daisies?" Edric looked up from the ground at his teacher with fire in his eyes. "And don't lose your temper. It only clouds your thinking and makes you too rash in your attack. I'm trying to save your life and your father the grief of losing you. Now, again!"

The attacks went on, swords raised; the clash of metal on metal as the lesson continued. Sweat was pouring from Edric's body and his arms could feel the burn of the weight of the sword and shield. His mail shirt hung heavily on his body over the padded undercoat. His legs were weary with the constant feint, attack, feint, attack, spin, forward, backward, attack, duck. After what seemed an eternity the lesson ceased and he and Alaric took water from the bucket with a horn dipper.

Edric ladled the cool water over his head and then drank from the dipper; the water from his head mixing with what missed his mouth and flowed down his smooth chin and soaking into his clothes. "We'll take a bit of a break and start again." Alaric's voice was very serious.

Usually there was some joking taunts passed back and forth from the younger to the older man and back again, but today everything was serious and Edric didn't know why. They skirmished for another hour with only small intervals for water now and again until finally Alaric called a halt.

"Why are we training so hard and why are you so serious today?" Edric asked.

Alaric took a long look at his young pupil and in his rough brogue began, "Beorn, your father and my friend, is the king's Reeve, his district governor. This you know. Did you not see the messengers going in and out the gates for the last two days? War is brewing. King Athelstan has been working hard to unite his grandfather Alfred's kingdom under one ruler with the petty western kings of smaller fiefdoms, the northern war lords and the Norse-Irish invaders not liking it and threatening to rebel at every turn.

The accord agreed on by Constantine in Scotland is chaffing and he wants to be free of Athelstan and the peace has come to an end. We are going to war. This will be no minor skirmish between the king's men and some Viking raiders, but a pitched battle of thousands. I'm getting you ready for it. Battle is like nothing you have ever faced before. This battle will be unlike anything anyone has ever faced before. Each encounter will move slowly like the shadow on the sundial. It will seem like hours but it will take only a moment, decided in an instant with the stroke of a blade, the swing of an axe, the thrust of a spear, the flight of an arrow. Other than killing your first boar with a spear last year you have never faced someone trying to kill you. Well, in battle it happens over and over and over again. You take one man down, perhaps he is killed, perhaps he is only wounded, some filled with hate, some with fear, some with pride but all trying to do you harm. Then there is another and another one after that and you feel as though you could not lift your arm again or parry one more blow and you watch someone you know go down beside you but you keep on going because if you don't you'll be next.

Is any of this sinking into that thick head of yours? Am I talking to myself? This battle may very well be the biggest ever fought on our own soil and many will die. I don't want you to be one of them."

Edric's mouth went dry and the color drained from his face. Battles were something that happened somewhere else, isolated fights between raiders or the Irish seeking slaves; between a few dozen men on either side; tales of valor from the old lore. This was war. He was afraid, not only for himself, but for his father, his family, the King.

"They will make peace like the last time. The Scots, the Danes and the Irish always have. King Constantine II knows he cannot win by himself. Even I know that."

"Yes, boy, but it's not only him this time. His nephew is Owain of Cumbria, who is himself a new king and King Olaf of Ireland and Denmark is his son-in-law. No, there are three armies against two this time; Constantine's three against King Athelstan's armies of Wessex and Mercia. And they hate us, Boy. They hate us. Athelstan is changing everything. He loves learning and I believe he loves God as we do.

He wants everyone to learn to read and write. He has a vision for a united kingdom with one language and one ruler. He is a godly and pious man. He builds churches and funds scholars. He is well deserving of our loyalty, but he will change everything and the others don't like that. He wants law and justice. They want to loot, pillage and take as they please. He wants to protect the innocent. They want to slaughter them. So this isn't just about a battle. It's about life itself and how we live it. Now, that's enough sermonizing for one day. Go clean up Boy and head to your other lessons."

Edric made his way to his room in the keep. It was old, a mixture of stone and wood set on high ground. Bits of it went back to the Roman rule; at least some of the stones had Latin inscriptions cut into them. It was odd to see a Latin word carved in stone in the middle of a wall and wonder where the rest of it was set. The stone had been chosen because it fit the space. It was the same in the church. The chapel had been built out of the stone ruins of some Roman building left over when the emperor pulled all the soldiers off Hadrian's Wall 500 years ago.

He always thought it was funny to see a sundial cut into the lintel stone at the church entrance because he could always see how long the priest's homily had taken from the time he went in until the time he went out. He thought the builder had a secret sense of humor when he set that stone.

His feet scuffed through the rushes on the planked floor put down to keep out the cold of the coming winter through the bottom of leather boots. It was high fall now. Harvest was continuing and the reapers were in the fields. The leaves had turned and the air was growing crisp.

Edric was headed back to his room to clean up before the noon meal. His mail shirt and weapons he left at the armory. He was clad now in his padded jerkin. His arms were sore from training. He washed himself at the ewer and dried himself with one of the rough woven towels hanging on the iron hook beside the raised bowl. Edric had given the glowing brazier a stir as he came into the room. He changed quickly into a woven long green tunic and wrapped the leather belt around him fastening it with his silver headed serpent clasp.

He had slipped it through the leather loop in his dagger sheath and now his dagger hung by his side. Edric sat on the edge of his feather bed with his head in his hands and thought about what his teacher and mentor had said. "War!" He thought to himself. "War and fighting and death." He was not worried about death so much as about dying. He believed he would go to heaven when he died.

The memory of his mother's voice came back to him. They had been travelling in her wagon to the fair. His father was riding ahead with their guards and a much younger Alaric. His mother, Gwenhild travelled comfortably in her tapestry hung wagon ensconced on pillows with him beside her. They came to a crossroads and there had been a great carved stone cross there where the roads met.

"What is that, Mother?" His childish voice had asked.

"It is a cross, my son."

"What does it mean?"

"It is a symbol, a sign." His mother answered.

"Like a road sign? A symbol for what? Does it tell us how to get somewhere?"

His mother smiled. "So many questions, young one. It is a symbol and a sign as well. Certainly it will help you on your path. Many years ago there was a man named Jesu, Jesus. He lived in the Holy Land in the east and he was the Son of God."

"I know of him. We learned of Him at church from Father Anselm."

"Yes, it is the same man." She said.

"He turned water into wine, opened the eyes of a blind man and even fed five thousand people from five loaves and two fish that a little boy gave to the disciples. I gave my fish to Father Anselm last week, but I think he just fed himself." His young voice trilled. His mother smiled again.

"Yes. Jesus did all those things. Did Father Anselm tell you what happened to him?"

"No, we haven't gotten to that part of the story yet."

"Well, this man, Jesus who had never sinned, never did anything wrong, died on a cross to pay our debt of sin to God the Father and that cross reminds us of what He did and how much we need Him.

You know about sin don't you?"

"I know I disobey some times and that is a sin."

"Yes, well, we've all disobeyed. We've all broken God's law."

"Even Father . . . even . . . you?" He remembered his mother's smile when he asked her that.

"Yes, even me." "So we all should have been on a cross?"

His mother grew silent for a moment and then spoke, "Yes, yes, there should have been a cross for every person that ever walked the earth because we have all sinned and cannot reach up to God, but He reached down to us. Jesus died for us in our place, for all of us, there was only one cross. The others are a reminder of what He has done."

"So what do I have to do?" He asked.

"Do?"

"Yes, mother, what do I have to do to get Jesus to take my cross?"

She smiled again. "Believe. Believe that He died in our place and ask Him to take your place."

"Right now?"

"If you like." His mother said.

"Out loud?"

"It needn't be aloud. Only if you want to."

Edric remembered how he had bowed his head and silently mouthed the words as best he understood to ask Jesus to take his place. He remembered the peace that filled his young heart and filled it still, at least until Alaric started talking about war. There was a lot of pain between dying and dead in war and that gave him pause. He'd seen men who'd lost limbs or an eye in battle; scarred for life. Some of them begged at the gates of the town. Others were objects of scorn and laughter because of their disfigurement.

After the meal Edric finished his other lessons for the day working with the tutors his father had brought in to teach him mathematics, Latin, Welsh, French and the language of the Vikings.

"Know how to talk to your enemy, son." His father had said when he asked why he was learning these languages. He completed his other subjects and went down to the great hall for the evening meal. He noticed as he walked the rush strewn flagstones the worried looks on the servants who passed him. He saw the messengers coming and going from his father's rooms like bees to the hive. There was a tension in the air that he had never felt before. The hall was full of strangers; men with stern and battle scarred faces: men who never smiled.

He caught fragments of their conversations. Kings Constantine, Olaf and Owain were frequently mentioned. He heard the words, "appeasement" and the French "parle´". He heard "battle" and "gathering armies". Several times he caught his father looking at him with an intense gaze that turned away as soon as Edric was aware of it.

With the meal over some of the men went off to their rooms, but others stayed by the main hearth or the braziers set in the floor and spoke quietly but intently among themselves; the flames throwing a golden haze on the smoke caught in the rafters.

His father held himself aloof from these conversations and would not be drawn in from their oblique questions. Edric just listened, not knowing which way the wind blew or what his father really thought. The days passed. Alaric filled each of them with his battle training; the rest with schooling.

Edric's arms were filling out and whatever baby fat left on his body was gone. He moved easily with his sword and axe. Holding his shield was second nature to him now. He was becoming a warrior.

The lands surrounding the keep filled with the tents of the gathering army, banners flying over each one like poppies in a meadow. There were hundreds now that had to be fed and kept. There were horses picketed in long lines in the fields. Wrapped in his long cloak Edric walked through the camp listening to voices from all over England.

He heard the soft rolling brogue of the Welsh from the far side of Offa's dyke; the harsh sharp accents of London and the broad vowels of Devon. Each night his father entertained the leaders of these men in the great hall; assessing, listening, discerning.

Edric found himself doing the same as he watched these men trying to gain influence with his father, trying to get more for themselves, trying to manipulate his father. One or two of them even tried it with him. He got very good at playing the careless young man until they stopped taking him seriously. Word got around.

Every day with Alaric was a lesson in statecraft as well as sword play and Edric was learning; growing wiser as well as stronger. Alaric shared his faith, his knowledge and his wisdom as they dueled day after grueling day. The day came when Edric arrived for his lesson that his father was there in the training ground in his mail with his great sword. Edric settled his helmet on his head, took hold of his shield and sword but when he stepped into the fighting circle it was not Alaric who faced him but his father. The lesson began slowly each taking the measure of the other. He had never faced a great sword before. His father handled it as if it were nothing. As the lesson went along his father began to press him more and more. The sheer weight of the great sword was enough to disarm him had he not gripped his own weapon all the tighter.

His father's face held no expression. No smile, no grimace, not even any strain. Then the pace picked up until the blows were flying so quickly it was hard to see the weapons except for the light flashing on the blades and the frozen tableau made whenever Edric caught the great blade on his shield or the hilts of his own sword.

Forward and back in a wild and dangerous Morris dance until the fear and frustration began to tell on Edric. "What was his father trying to do?" He thought. Every feint, every attack his father met and quelled; the great sword like a wall between them.

Then he saw his chance. His father had swung the blade through the air to bring it down on Edric's shield, Edric pushed it wide and rushed in close to his father under the blade and put his sword tip to his father's neck. His father smiled but looked up. Edric's eyes followed his father's and he saw that what he thought would have been a successful attack would have ended with both of their deaths. His father's armored gauntlets wrapped around his sword hilts where poised above Edric's head. He would have been crushed even had his sword struck home.

He dropped his head, but instead of berating him, his father embraced him and smiled. "Well done, my son. Well done. You have learned well. Now, go and change for your other lessons. We will speak later." His father nodded to the smiling Alaric and left. Edric was smiling as well. He knew he had passed some test. He just wasn't sure just what it was. "Well done, Boy!" Alaric exclaimed. "Well done!"

That night after the evening meal Edric strode through the great hall searching for his father. No one could tell Edric where he was, not even his mother Gwenhild. After a fruitless search through the keep and the great hall, Edric found himself outside the fortress palings at the chapel entrance staring at the old sundial set into the stone; its shadow now following the moonlight. He heard his father's voice coming through the small arched window in the door.

At first Edric thought there was someone else with his father and they were discussing something, arguing over something. He had rarely heard his father speak so intensely. Edric listened, waiting for the discussion to end before he entered.

Then he heard his own name. Slowly he lifted the latch that held the door and silently entered the room. He could see no one but his father. There he was on his knees at the altar hands clasped, head bowed with tears in his voice as he prayed aloud for his son. Edric went to the nearest bench and sat bowing his own head out of respect.

His father's words washed over him echoing in the cavernous stone chapel. He heard his father's words of pleading and love addressed to "Abba Father" just as if his father were talking to a real person not the air above the altar. Edric had never heard his father pray like this. Grace before a meal he had heard. Prayers with him at night as a child Edric remembered, but this was something else.

His father, like Jacob of old seemed to be wrestling with God. He heard his father's "amen" and watched him rise slowly from his knees. His father started when he saw Edric there on the bench. "Have you been here long?" His father asked.

"I was looking for you and had tried everywhere else. I heard your voice: saw that you were alone and came in to wait."

His father nodded. They were both standing awkwardly not quite looking at each other. "What is on your mind?"

His father said. "Please, sit."

They sat, not side by side, but his father straddling a bench in the front row his long dagger angling down to the flagstone floor; turning himself to face his son in the second row; Edric leaned forward arms on his knees.

"Is there going to be war, Father?"

"Oh yes. The kings in the north have been raiding the border cities for the last month. Every day brings news of their atrocities. Athelstan many think has been slow to respond, but he has been gathering the army until there is a force large enough to meet Olaf, Owain and Constantine. He knew a skirmish for a border town would not solve the problem. The King has a vision for the future. The lesser kings, warlords and chieftains want the old ways to continue and will not be subdued."

"What will you do?" Edric asked.

"I am the King's Reeve. I will follow the King as my father and grandfather followed Athelstan's Grandfather Alfred and his father, Edward. I will follow him because it is my duty, but I follow him more because it is right. What he wants is right and so I will follow him."

"And there will be war?"

"Yes, there will be war." "And there will be killing?"

"Yes, people will die; unless the others yield and they are too full of their own importance to do that. People will die, perhaps a great many of them I am sorry to say. There is news that the Danes from Ireland sailed to Scotland and made their way south over water; landing in the northwest. We must meet this force to protect the kingdom. We will need every man and so I am asking you to join us. It will be dangerous, even deadly."

"I will go with you. I will follow you." Edric spoke the words to his father evenly.

"It is not enough for you to follow me; as much as I appreciate that, but you must follow the king. He is our ruler, our liege lord.

It is he who will lead this battle. It is he who will lead England."

"I will follow him, Father even though I do not know him. I have never met him. I know only what Alaric has shared with me, but I also know that you follow him; that will be enough for me."

His father dropped his head and felt the weight of his son's choice on his shoulders. He took a long slow breath and began, "Word has come that the Irish and Scottish flotillas have set sail. We will gather our army as we go. Since he became king Athelstan has organized garrisons a day's ride apart to protect the surrounding towns and villages across the southland. We will meet Constantine with roughly fifteen thousand men against their fifteen thousand by all accounts. We head for the northwest near the Scottish border by the coast. Rest tonight. Tomorrow we ride."

His father laid his hand on Edric's shoulder and squeezed it gently. Edric could feel the warmth of his father's hands through the rough fabric of his tunic. He felt the love and concern as well.

Edric's mother was packing his things into a trunk when he arrived at his room. From the doorway he watched her fold each item carefully and place it gently in the ironbound wooden trunk that would go on the wagons that followed the army. She was humming softly. He recognized the tune as a chant in Latin. For a moment he just stood and watched her, listening to her clear soft voice. She held a bittersweet smile on her lips. She pressed one of his shirts that she had woven for him to her lips and put it in the trunk. She finished packing as he watched and closed and latched the trunk.

"You knew I would choose to go then?"

"Yes. I believed you would. You are becoming a man with a man's choices. Choosing to follow the King with all that means is a man's choice, a woman's too come to that. I too have fought the raiders as a young warrior maiden in my time although I used a bow to defend our village, not a blade. I know what awaits you. What you do is right. I am at peace with your choice."

"You fought? You killed?"

"Yes." His mother replied sadly. "I was just your age. My father was the local chieftain, your grandsire for whom you are named. He taught me to hunt and shoot as well as to read alongside my brothers, your uncles. So when the alarm was sounded and everyone grabbed their bows and arrows I took my quiver and bow along with the others. Your grandfather took a look at me and then said, 'Come. We will need every bow. Mind you have your dagger as well, if you are captured.' My hands were shaking so I could hardly nock the arrow, but then I saw one of the marauders grab a small girl and before I could think I had loosed an arrow and saw it pierce his throat. He let go the girl and fell like a stone. And then there were other lives to save and others to take. It seemed the work of a moment but we were at it most of the night; caring for the wounded, putting out the fires, burying the dead. By morning we were exhausted, but the village was safe again. It was not the only time."

Edric was silent for a moment picturing his mother as a fierce warrior maiden. Then he spoke, "Mother, I do have a question."

"Yes?"

"We have spoken of spiritual things, things of the church, of the Lord, but how does war fit in with what Jesus says about turning the other cheek and not defending yourself?"

"That is a theologian's question, but I will tell you what I think. When I fought the raiders with the bow it was not to defend myself, but our village. Your father has also fought in his time to protect those in need of a champion and now as he goes to war and you with him. It is to defend those who cannot defend themselves. It is to protect the village from being raided, the maidens from harm, the children from being taken and sold as slaves. Might does not make right, but it may require might to defend what is right. That is the best answer my wit can give you." He nodded silently. With that she took his head in her hands and kissed him on his forehead, "God go with you, my son." And she left.

Edric paced about the room for a bit and then readied himself for bed. He lay awake on his mattress long into the night, his thoughts in turmoil for the coming battle. Would he be brave? Would he be able to defend the king? Would he survive the battle?

Edric would doze and awaken from some fresh apparition of battle and death; over and over again in fitful sleep until the dawn began to show in the window of his rooms.

He finally arose splashed himself awake with the water in his ewer and dressed himself for travel. His baggage was already taken by the servants. He had his sword belt and sword with him in his room. He strapped them on over his tunic and went to meet his father to break his fast. He might not be able to sleep soundly, but he found he could eat.

After breaking his fast with his father and the other leaders riding with them to meet Constantine's army, Edric sought out his mother to bid her farewell. She was somber and silent as he kissed her cheek and held her hands in parting. Life was hard and sometimes short. She knew no good would come of wailing and tears. It was in God's hands now; her son, her husband, the King and the men who followed him were all in God's hands. She went to the palisade gate to watch the army ride away.

The procession's slow progress wound its way through the valley until she could see only the blurred shapes of the luggage wagons through her tears. When she could no longer see them, she turned and went to her rooms with her needle work to await her long and lonely vigil. Many days would pass before there would be news.

Twenty miles was as much as the army could hope to travel on a good day to arrive at the meeting strong enough to fight and it would take them many days before they would join the other elements of King Athelstan's army and face the Danes, the Scots and the Irish on the Wirral. It was mid-September and the days were growing cooler and shorter. By the third day the pattern of making camp, training with Alaric, eating, more training, sleep, breaking camp and journeying on had set itself. Edric said little as he rode in the vanguard with his father.

Alaric was there riding close to Edric's father, Beorn, ever watchful for the hidden blade, the arrow's flight. Edric listened to the conversations of the men around him. Some were joking; some made coarse talk; a show of bravery by men afraid of dying.

There were bitter words for those on the other side of the border who had broken the peace and bold guesses at Athelstan's battle plan on a peninsula filled with the enemy. The days passed slowly with the wearying journey. Each day the foresters and huntsmen would seek out fuel and food for the massive army that flowed like the tide across the fields and forests of England.

Each day when the horses had been seen to and the camp pitched Edric and Alaric would train, occasionally joined by his father and his great sword. Watching his father and Alaric train was more like watching a chess match than the all-out sword clashing bouts between Edric and his mentor.

After what seemed like an age to Edric the column of riders and men reached the King and his army in the northwest of England near the marshy stretches of the Wirral. When they crested the low hills that surrounded the plain like the lip of a bowl Edric could see the army laid out before him with tents and banners like a city made of cloth. The wind blew strong and cold across the water. Even the low trees were shaped by the constant wind.

They made their way to the outward edges still unoccupied with tents and once again began to make camp. A messenger came to his father from the King. Beorn read it and said to Edric "Make yourself presentable and come with me. Quickly! Athelstan does not like to be kept waiting."

Edric got down from his horse and hit his dusty tunic with his gauntlets a few times and ran his fingers through his hair. That was the extent of his grooming. His father gave a small chuckle and turned on his heel. Edric began to follow rapidly behind him. They threaded their way through the mass of men and animals until they found themselves at the opening of a large tent with sumptuous banners floating in the sky above them. They were announced by the servant sent to fetch them and left at the entrance to the King's tent. Edric took one more look at himself and took another swat with the leather gauntlets. He licked his lips and swallowed hard. "In you go!" His father said. Edric walked between the armed sentries into the presence of the king.

At first glance the tent had a sectioned wooden floor. Candle stands stood in the four corners of the room and there was another lamp suspended from cross members in the ceiling. There was a bronze ewer in one corner and a glowing brazier in another. An ornate cot ran along one side of the large tent set in the midst of heavy bed curtains to keep in the heat and keep out the light. The tent was redolent with some kind of incense that wafted through the air from a small burner on its own stand.

Athelstan sat on a raised platform in an elaborately carved chair. His simple crown glinted on his reddish blonde head. His beard was full, but it did not cover the bejeweled chain around his neck. The famous golden hilted sword given to him by his grandfather, King Alfred, stretched across the table before him. Also on the table were several maps drawn on vellum held open by a jeweled dagger on one side and an ink pot on the other. Several heavily bound books with beautifully embossed bindings lay haphazardly on the desk as if the king had been reading them one after another.

Athelstan rose when the men had entered and stepped in front of the oak table. Edric wasn't sure what to do. He took a side-long glance at his father who was bowing and so he bowed, again watching his father to see just how low and how long he should bow before the king. Athelstan motioned for them to rise.

The king smiled and grasped Beorn's forearm pulling him toward him in a strong clasp of hands. "It is good to see you again, Beorn, my friend. I hope you have had a safe journey."

"All went well, my liege. May I present my son, Edric." Athelstan appraised Edric for a moment before he spoke.

"There is a light of intelligence in your eyes, young man. Have you education?" Edric hesitated. "You may speak."

Edric cleared his throat. His first words came out as a kind of creaking falsetto reminiscent of his voice change. "Sire. . . . Sire my father believes education is a good thing."

"So it is. It has fallen on hard times of late. Some of our priests cannot read or write, not to mention the majority of our people.

How are we to learn and follow God if we cannot read His word? I am proposing a translation of the Holy Scriptures in our common tongue so that all Englishmen who can read can read the scriptures for themselves. I'm not sure how it will fare with the church. So you read?"

"Yes, Sire."

"Languages?"

"Sire, again my father believes one should know the language of the enemy and so I speak the language of the Vikings, but I speak the language of the French as well and Latin. I am also studying the language of our neighbors the Welsh."

"Well done, young man. Do you read them as well?"

"Yes, Sire."

"Here, let me show you something." Athelstan grabbed Edric by the sleeve and pulled him around the desk. He picked up one of the books, flipped the clasp and gently opened the book. Edric saw it was an illustrated manuscript in Latin, beautifully colored and finely drawn.

Athelstan thrust it in his hands. Edric began to read in the Latin, translating in his mind as he went. It was from the Bible, an account of the battles of the Hebrew people. "I find that the Hebrews were very good at battle plans, the man Joshua in particular, King David too. So I look to them for inspiration when I go into battle. What do you think?" Edric read on.

It was a record of a battle in which the Israelites had pretended to be defeated and ran. When the enemy pursued them, other warriors in hiding closed in on the enemy and defeated them.

"That sounds like a very wise plan, Sire. Very cunning."

"Yes, that's what I thought and since our opponents don't read and they certainly don't read the Bible, I think it will be a surprise to them. But you must keep that information to yourself. Here."

Athelstan reached another smaller volume from his desk. It was beautifully bound in embossed leather stained blue and chased with gold over wooden covers with a gold clasp on the slim volume.

"It is the Gospel of St. John. I wish for you to have it. I treasure learning and those who are willing to learn. My gift to you. The Lord be with you as we go to battle. And now, my young friend, you must excuse me, but the pressures of the kingdom intrude."

The King nodded to Edric and his father they turned and made their way back to their own men and camp. "Well, now you have met the king." Edric's father said. "What did you think?" He could see the light of hero worship already in his son's eyes.

"I don't know what to think. Whatever I was expecting he is not it." Edric ran his hands over the beautiful leather of his book. "I supposed from what Alaric had said and from the things I heard you and the others discussing around the table I thought he would be smaller and perhaps a little bent over from learning. Someone more like a scholar, or at least what I think of as a scholar. More like Father Anselm. Athelstan is more like I think King David must have looked."

"Yes and we are going to slay a giant named Constantine." His father replied. "Get your cloak. We shall walk among the men."

Edric fetched his cloak from his baggage and with his father began to walk through the camp. Alaric followed at a discreet distance. His father would step into a group of men and ask after their journey, their families, their needs. He did this over and over again. Some of the men he knew better than others, but each group received attention. Edric followed silently; watching, listening as they went from group to group, campfire to campfire. They returned to their own tent.

"Tomorrow we will ride to meet the enemy. An army this size cannot stay in one place too long. The countryside will not sustain it. All the wood gets burned and the game eaten and there was not much here to start with."

"Will there be fighting tomorrow?" Edric asked as he prepared for bed. His own cot looked very welcoming.

"Probably not. We will ride out to meet Constantine, Olaf and Owain. There will be delegations sent back and forth. There will probably be some show of attack. There will definitely be taunts and insults shouted back and forth between the men. There always are. After that we will see. My son, the king gave you a book.

I too have some learning and this is something I translated from the Latin when I was your age. I have written it out for you, but I have it in my head from memory. It is from the Psalms. It is the ninety-first Psalm. I hope it will be as encouraging and comforting to you as it has been to me."

His father handed him a piece of parchment with the words inscribed upon it. Then his father began to quote: *1 ¶ He who is dwelling In the secret place of the Most High, In the shade of the Mighty lodgeth habitually, 2 He is saying of Jehovah, 'My refuge, and my bulwark, my God, I trust in Him, 3 For He delivereth thee from the snare of a fowler, From a calamitous pestilence. 4 With His pinion He covereth thee over, And under His wings thou dost trust, A shield and buckler is His truth. 5 Thou art not afraid of fear by night, Of arrow that flieth by day, 6 Of pestilence in thick darkness that walketh, Of destruction that destroyeth at noon, 7 There fall at thy side a thousand, And a myriad at thy right hand, Unto thee it cometh not nigh. 8 But with thine eyes thou lookest, And the reward of the wicked thou seest, 9 ¶ (For Thou, O Jehovah, art my refuge,) The Most High thou madest thy habitation.*

10 Evil happeneth not unto thee, And a plague cometh not near thy tent, 11 For His messengers He chargeth for thee, To keep thee in all thy ways, 12 On the hands they bear thee up, Lest thou smite against a stone thy foot. 13 On lion and asp thou treadest, Thou trampest young lion and dragon. 14 Because in Me he hath delighted, I also deliver him — I set him on high, Because he hath known My name. 15 He doth call Me, and I answer him, I am with him in distress, I deliver him, and honour him. 16 With length of days I satisfy him, And I cause him to look on My salvation!'

Paul wrote to Timotheus, his son in the ministry, "'God hath not given us the spirit of fear, but of power and of love and of a sound mind.' Tomorrow we go out to meet the enemy. Very soon there will be fighting, perhaps not tomorrow as I said, but soon. Whatever occurs, God will be with you. I will be in the vanguard with the King. You and Alaric with you will be a part of the army that hides until the trap is sprung. My son, these words do not come easily for me because it is not our way to wear our hearts on our sleeves, but I love you, I love you."

Edric looked at his father and then embraced him. "I love you too, my father." They made themselves ready for bed. His father blew out the lamp and they slept.

All too soon for Edric his father shook him gently awake. They broke their fast with some cold meats, cheese and bread and began to ready themselves for battle. Alaric came in to help each of them get into the padded jerkin and pull the chainmail over their heads. Over that came a tabard that marked them as the king's men. A simple bowl shaped helmet over the chainmail hood finished their armor.

Edric remembered Alaric's words about the helmet with the nose piece. "It's like a handle for your enemy. If he gets that close, and chances are he will, he can grab that and swing you about like a cat. Keep your sight free and protect your nose . . . along with the rest of your young hide." Edric smiled at this memory and wondered if he would smile again for the next few days. Dawn came cloaked in the peaty campfires of thirty thousand men. Beorn mounted his enormous black stallion from a block and rode to join the King. Alaric and Edric would be on foot.

They joined the others of his father's men and made their way silently to the copse of low trees stunted by the constant sea breeze from the north. There was no talking or jesting now, just the soft chink of chainmail and the whisper of leather as they moved through the trees. Athelstan had given orders that those with him in the forefront were to spread out to give the appearance of a larger group and yet let those who noted such things see that there were not so many of the king's men as there were of the enemy.

As the sun rose on the cold October morning Edric could see the clouds of breath from the nostrils of the great horses in the distance. He felt the ground shake as the riders on their massive mounts moved slowly into place. In spite of the cold he was sweating. He looked at Alaric and saw his battle face.

There was a stern rictus on his countenance. No emotion showed. His eyes were fixed on the distance and only the slightest movement of his lips as he breathed showed that Alaric was animate at all. The two armies were in place facing one another. All was silent.

Then there was a clash of sword on shield loud enough to wake the dead and terrible in its knolling boom from Constantine's men. There were at first harsh shouts from their enemy answered by Athelstan's men in their own low call with an echoing crash of their own. And then the taunts began. Edric had not known such words to exist and he blushed under his armor to hear what the enemy was saying about Athelstan's lineage, his manhood, his red beard.

There came answering threats from Athelstan's men with equal ferocity. And it went on and on and on throughout the day as Edric and Alaric and the men with them hidden in the trees remained silent and slowly grew colder and colder. Just before dark there was a charge from the Scots and the Danes that caught Athelstan's men by surprise and some were killed and wounded.

A shout went up as the Danes and Scots pulled back one of them carrying high on a spear the severed head of one of Athelstan's men. Then darkness fell and both sides returned to their camps for the night. This was the way war was waged.

The night passed slowly and there was little said between father and son as they went through the motions of the evening like automatons. There in the darkness as they lay in their cots, Beorn's voice came quietly out of the darkness. "I love you, son."

"I love you, Father." Came Edric's answer and all was quiet.

Again the daybreak came quickly and quietly for Edric as they made ready for battle. "Today, there will be an attack. Athelstan will provoke them. When the horns sound you will close in the trap Athelstan has designed. Remember what Alaric has taught you. Remember that God is with you. Remember I love you." With that Beorn mounted his steed and rode off to join the King in his vanguard with the others on horseback.

Alaric laced him into his mail and they set out like the day before to the low woods. Again all was silent except for the murmuring sound of two thousand men moving as quietly as they may through the woods. Edric knew there were another two thousand in the copse across from the open field where yesterday's show had taken place and today's preliminaries were beginning.

All began as it had the day before with the clashing of shields and the threats and taunts across the open space, but when the sun was up and strong in the eyes of the enemy facing east Athelstan struck. There was a flight of arrows to darken the sky. Edric heard the shrieks of those who could not get under the shield wall or those whose necks had been found through the spaces by the silent arrows of Athelstan's archers. Then Athelstan's army began to charge. The Danes and Scots lowered the long pointed spears to stave off the men on horseback.

The enemy gave a great shout and ran to meet the attack. Edric could hear the guttural roar of the men. Some were shouting battle cries of "Constantine!" or "Owain!" Others were swearing in Danish with their long plaited beards tucked into their leather armor swinging their axes and war hammers over their heads. There was a clash as the two armies met like the breaking of a wave upon the rocks of the sea. The air was split by the sound of metal on metal intermingled with the cries and shouts Edric could not understand.

Still Athelstan's men on either side of the battle line stayed silent and still so their position would not be betrayed by the flash of a blade or the sound of a voice. Then the king's men in the forefront began to fall back, some turning and running.

There was a victorious shout from the bloodthirsty Danes and fierce Scots behind them as they began to pursue. The Irish were in full cry as well. It was as if a floodgate had burst and let in the flood tide of the enemy pursuit of Athelstan's beleaguered men. The chase went on for nearly half a mile allowing all Constantine's army to come between the jaws of the trap.

When Constantine himself with Kings Owain and Olaf brought up the rear of the flow with their banners and personal guard the horns began to blow. There was a loud clear call from the deep booming horns and in an instant Edric, Alaric and all those with them began to close in on the unwary pursuers. There was a flight of arrows from the hidden archers that found its way into the exposed backs of the enemy dogging the retreat. Then the jaws of the trap began to close.

The charge began slowly, picking up speed as those in the front found their feet and judged their path. Those following then could also pick up their speed and soon the two sides of the trap were converging quickly on the right and left flanks of the enemy.

Those at the rear of Constantine's charge were caught completely unaware. Stragglers were cut down and silenced quickly. Then the onslaught caught up with the main body of the enemy. Someone must have turned to look behind them because there suddenly arose a shout of warning that spread as Constantine's army lost its momentum and began circling to protect the kings. A fire arrow went up from the archers with Edric to signal to Athelstan that the trap had been sprung and those running must now turn and fight.

A shield wall began to form in front of Edric, Alaric and those with them. Edric brought his sword down on the shoulder of one Dane who could not get his shield arm up quickly enough to ward off the blow. The man went down and Edric went on to the next man in front of him.

His arm raised and dropped in deadly action against those before him. All the days of fighting with Alaric made the motion almost without thought. His shield came up to ward off a blow and then his sword struck home under the guard of the blonde Norseman before him. His eyes slid sideways for a moment and there was Alaric in a fury swinging his battle axe to cut down another enemy. Alaric caught Edric's eye and he shouted, "Pay attention, you young fool! Don't stand there gauping!" Edric caught himself just in time to fend off another blow from a war hammer. He countered and cut the man down hitting him with the edge of his shield. All this seemed to be happening in some exaggerated slow motion like running in deep water. It seemed as if each action, each motion was set apart in its clarity and focus. He saw blows coming and dodged them. He swung his sword and moved on over and over just as Alaric had said.

They had driven a wedge in the shield wall dividing the protection that was supposed to be for the usurping kings. The breach was growing ever wider as the men with Edric filled the gap like a flood.

Suddenly, standing before him was a giant Viking with a great sword held in his hand like a twig. The sword came down on Edric's shield and shattered it like crockery.

He still held the handles of the broken pieces in his hand, the shield flapping uselessly in shards. He moved in close as he had with his father and slashed his sword across the leather covering the man's great chest. His sword cut the leather and drew blood. The man roared in a rage and brought his hilts down on Edric's helm. In an instant of clarity Edric could smell the man's foul breath and the stench of his body. Edric dodged but still the glancing blow left Edric stunned. He couldn't see or move for a moment. He felt his knees give way. The world grew silent as sense and reason left him.

There came in the stillness his father's voice, *"4 With His pinion He covereth thee over, And under His wings thou dost trust, A shield and buckler is His truth. 5 Thou art not afraid of fear by night, Of arrow that flieth by day, 6 Of pestilence in thick darkness that walketh, Of destruction that destroyeth at noon, 7 There fall at thy side a thousand, And a myriad at thy right hand, Unto thee it cometh not nigh."*

The world was tilting. He felt as if he were seeing it at the end of a long tunnel. He was on his knees his arms down, his sword tip on the ground. He looked up watching the mighty sword falling to cleave him in two in one long slow motion. It grew ever closer and he could do nothing to stop it or save himself. "I am going to die." He thought.

He began slowly to drop his head lower to avoid the blow and yet he knew it would not be enough. As he was moving he saw the man's bloodshot eyes turn away from him, the arc of the sword began to waiver. A blade came through the air over Edric's head and caught the giant in the chest. The man was felled like a great oak. Edric registered the look of surprise in the man's eyes as the life flowed out of him.

His hands still gripped the mighty sword now useless. Edric felt a hand grab his arm and pull him up. He could see Alaric shouting at him shaking him, but he could hear nothing. They were in a small bubble of peace in the midst of chaos and destruction that was going on all around them. Edric slowly got to his feet. He took a deep breath and reason began to return.

The battle began to come back to him and he gathered himself once again. It seemed as if it took an eternity, but he knew it could only be seconds of time. He saw the worry on Alaric's face. He saw the fear for him and the slight smile that began as Alaric recognized Edric was shaken but not injured. The smile turned to pain as another warrior slid his blade under Alaric's arm were there was no mail. Alaric spun and jerked away pulling the sword from the man's grasp as he moved and swung his ax to kill the man who had stabbed him in the back, but then Alaric faltered and dropped to one knee. Panic and fear seized Edric. This could not be. His mentor, his protector could not be harmed. He could not be wounded. This was Alaric! Alaric was down now.

His arm reached up to grasp Edric. "Follow the King! Follow the King! Follow the King!" Alaric's eyes closed and he was gone. Edric knelt in the midst of the maelstrom that swirled around him for a moment, making a silent prayer for strength and then he gathered himself picked up his sword and entered the torrent of battle again. He lost all track of the passage of time. It seemed as if his entire life had been spent on this field of blood. His arm rose and fell without thought.

He found another shield from some other fallen warrior and fought on. The shield walls surrounding the kings had broken. Small groups of the invaders were fighting their way to the edges of the battle and running for their boats dropping weapons as they fled. The English pursued them cutting them down along the line of retreat.

Edric found himself with the pursuers at the water's edge watching the nearly empty ships of the enemy pull from the shore with barely enough men to row them away. Flights of arrows followed them until the long boats were out of range. A proud fleet of thousands had landed; a ragged few were sailing away. A great weariness engulfed him.

He began to look around him at the men who stood beside him. He saw the blood and the wounds that none yet felt. Then he saw Athelstan and his father on their chargers with the others in Athelstan's retinue, but the numbers were fewer than when they had set out on that crisp October morning that seemed years ago now. Many were the fallen. The black dog of battle had begun to settle on those who lived. They had won the war, but the cost had been great.

Edric's father saw him and leaned in to ask the King's permission to go to him. Edric saw the crowned head nod once and the king's eyes fell on him. Athelstan smiled wearily and nodded his thanks and acknowledgement to a fellow survivor.

Edric lifted his eyes again to the horizon where the ships of his enemies were disappearing in the distance. England would be united north to south, east to west. Athelstan's vision would come true. Owain, Olaf and Constantine were limping back to their own countries. Their armies broken. Their greed and pride had cost them five princes, seven barons. Out of the cohort of fifteen thousand only three thousand returned to Scotland and Ireland. The kings had each lost sons, brothers, nephews on the blood soaked ground of the Wirral.

Beorn got down wearily from his sweat stained mount. Edric turned to his father and embraced him. The weariness overtook him and he began to sob in great gulping gasps as the emotions of the day swept over him. His father held him close and let the tears fall. "Alaric?"

"Dead." Edric croaked, "He died saving me. I should have been quicker. I should have been better. I . . . should have . . . I wanted. . . I watched him die. I could not stop his wound. He had saved me. I could not save him."

"Peace, my son. Peace. He died in grace protecting one he loved as if you were his own son. He would not change places with you now for all the accolades of battle. We will find his body. We will bury him. We will mourn him. We will remember his sacrifice. We will keep faith with his memory. Come." The two warriors, father and son, leading the great black stallion, made their way through the ruin of battle to the place where Alaric's body lay.

They found him easily enough His body was not disturbed. Already the carrion beasts were beginning to come to the field, circling in the dulling sky that the setting sun had turned to blood. The air was filled with the moans and cries of the wounded from both sides. The infirmarians from the monasteries were seeing to them. These holy brothers had followed the army knowing they would be needed when the fighting was over.

They were binding wounds; doling out sips of poppy juice to those in great pain and to others with no hope of recovery. Other priests were praying over the dead.

Beorn saw two of his own men picking their way through the bodies looking for their own dead. He called to them and gave orders that they were to find a litter and bear Alaric's body to a place where he could be buried. They would find a priest and have a service. There would be others who would not return to their village who would be mourned as well. It seemed an age since dawn had come that morning and yet darkness had not fallen on this October day. Both men felt spent, empty.

Edric looked out over the field of the fallen and knew he would remember this day for the rest of his life. He took off his helmet and saw the crease the great sword had caused and realized just how close he had come to death.

They returned to their tent to wash and don clean tunics for Alaric's service. Edric finished before his father and sat on his cot turning the pages of the book the king had presented to him. His eyes fell on a passage near the end.

He began to translate it from the Latin; "I am the resurrection and the life. He that believeth in me though he were dead, yet shall he live and whosoever believeth in me shall never die." The tears rolled down his face again because he knew he would see Alaric again one day. "I will read this at his service." He thought.

Darkness had fallen by the time all was ready. By torchlight they laid Alaric to rest. The priest said his words over him and then Beorn spoke and finally Edric read from the Book of John the King had given him. Each took a wooden spade of dirt and filled in the grave in turn. They returned to their tent and the weariness of the day overtook them.

The sun was quite high when Edric woke the next day. It took a moment for him to remember where he was and why he was here. The events of the battle swarmed in on him and he was almost overcome. His father came in with some food and Edric's world began to right itself again. He was sore. His body was covered in bruises and he had no memory of how he had received them. His superficial cuts had been dresses and he showed very little damage from the day before.

His father had a few cuts from blades that had made their way past his chain mail but he too was little hurt.

"We have been summoned to see the King. Dress yourself and we will go. In Athelstan's compassion he told me not to wake you, but come when you were ready. Not all kings are so nice minded."

Once again they were announced. Athelstan looked much the same as he had on their first meeting; perhaps a little darker about the eyes. Once again he stood and came around in front of the table laden with maps and books and again Athelstan greeted them warmly.

"Young man, you have served me well. You have fought bravely, more bravely than many your senior. You are young and have your life before you. I have many boons within my power to grant. Your father is my Reeve and I would have you follow in his footsteps if you will. But what now is your wish."

"Sire, yesterday was a day of darkness and light for me. Light because the battle was won, your crown secured and our nation united, but dark because one dear to me was lost in the battle. If I may be bold in my youth I will let his last words guide me in my choice."

"Young man, do not hesitate to share these words. I shall not stop your tongue. Speak freely."

"Alaric was my teacher, my mentor, my friend, my brother in grace. He held you in high regard. His dying words as he breathed his last were these, 'Follow the King!' And so I would, Sire, all the days of my life. I shall follow the King."

THE END

6
THE DAGGER

The dagger lay on the ground in all of its magnificent splendor. The deep blue sapphire held in the panther's mouth glowed in the light of the clear morning sun. At the hilts the rubies set at each cross piece held by a panther's claw evanesced from within as they nestled in the dew laden bracken. Even the golden amber eyes of the panther were testaments to the artisan's craft that cast the silver sinews that flowed across the hilt.

The blade was a thing of deadly beauty and extravagance. Malin could see in his mind's eye the minute scroll work on the slightly curved predatory blade now hidden by the blue calf skin that covered the bejeweled sheath. From the tear drop emerald held by a paw on the sheath to the silver bound fastenings that held the sapphire at the end of the hilt, the dagger was an object of immense worth and beauty. And now it was on the ground before him just as he had planned.

Malin had seen the dagger at his father's table the night before. Sir Isaac had used it to cut his venison and spear his potato. He had seen that Malin was fascinated by its beauty. When Sir Isaac finished eating he wiped the blade clean and held it out to Malin. Sir Isaac told the story of the knife. "When I was in the east during the third crusade under Richard the Lionhearted, a Saracen whose life I saved gave me this dagger. Like many things the crusade started for good reason, but greed and a desire for power turned it into something very different."

There were a few knowing nods from grayer heads around the table, but others frowned at the truth they found unpleasant. "It was a time apart for me." Sir Isaac said. "But what of the dagger? You can't stop with that. How did you come to save this man's life?" Malin's father, Godric had asked the question everyone else wanted to know. "As I said, he was a Saracen, a Moslem. He had been wounded by an arrow in the Saracen retreat from Acre. The arrow was still embedded in his thigh when I found him. He was very weak from loss of blood. I was making my way out of Acre toward Jaffa to join up with King Richard's army. I had a few yeomen with me, some archers, some pike men.

This man was hidden in the scrub on the side of the road when I heard his moan. I stopped, got down from my mount and with my great sword drawn began to look for the source of the sound. When I found him he had this dagger in his hand. He could hardly hold it. The tip wavered and dipped as he tried to defend himself. He was so weak, he was easily disarmed.

The men made camp while I cleaned his wound, cut the shaft from the arrow and pushed it through the leg and out the other side. He screamed and fainted from the pain and loss of blood.

Then I poured oil and wine into the wound, bound it up and waited to see if he would survive. It was a pleasant place with water and forage. We were in no particular hurry. Jaffa had been there three thousand years already. It wasn't going anywhere and I didn't know if we could find King Richard's army except by following the path of destruction left by every army since time began.

We made a litter for our patient and I dragged it behind my horse. Each day I gave him water and such food as he could and would eat according to what I knew about his religion. I kept the wound clean and changed the bandages. There were days when he was feverish and we had to soak cloths with water to keep him cool, but gradually he began to heal and talk. We came to an oasis and camped again. His fever had broken and the leg was mending, but still he could not walk.

He was possessed of some English and I had a little Arabic and between us we could communicate. After he got over his fear that we would torture him he began to tell me a little of himself. He was a warrior. His name is Abed Al-Azziz, it means 'servant of the powerful.' He had been in Egypt with Saladin and came north with his army.

Every day after he began to recover, he would unroll his prayer rug, turn toward Mecca and pray. Kneeling was bit difficult at first because of his wound. Once when he was struggling to get on his knees I helped him and he asked me why I would do such a thing. Actually he said, "Why do you help me, infidel?" When I laughed at that he asked me why I laughed. "Infidel means unfaithful. I have faith, just not in your Allah, but Jesus Christ." He was silent for a while after he finished his prayers and I knew more questions would come.

Each day we would speak more. Each day he would ask me about my faith, my belief, why I fought. Once he asked me why I had helped him when others would have either tortured him, killed him or left him to die slowly in the wilderness. "I am commanded to do so." I said. 'By King Richard?' "By Jesus Christ."

I said. "He commanded us to help the sick, the wounded, those in need, the hungry, the poor." 'Christian, I know of this prophet, Jesus, as you call him. It is said he was a good man.' I had moved from being an infidel, 'Christian, you are not like any I have ever met from the west.' "I am sorry," I said and meant it.

I had heard the stories of terrible things done in the name of Jesus Christ. The Master would not have acted so, but it would ever be the way of it. We are fallen humans in need of a Savior." Again older heads nodded around the table in the firelight and again others looked into their plates hearing what they did not wish to hear. "But the knife," Malin's father prodded. "One night as we camped I heard a muffled cry in the moonlight.

I arose with my sword in hand and began to steal softly through the camp. I looked to our guest and saw him half-sitting, completely still, unmoving. There before him was a desert cobra as long as my great sword, its head flared, its black scales like ebony shining in the moonlight, slowly weaving forward and back facing Azziz.

I had heard of this creature. Its venom was more powerful than the cobras of the east. Azziz was transfixed, afraid to move. I swung my blade swiftly in the silver light and cut the coiled serpent in half and I confess I kept on chopping at him until no part of him wriggled or moved."

There were a few throaty laughs and many smiles when Isaac said this. 'Christian,' Azziz said, 'you have twice saved my life and now it is yours.' Still shaking a little from the episode I said, "I know this is your custom, but I do not desire your life.

Azziz, what I have done for you, saving your life, this is what Jesus Christ has done for us. I know that your belief is about what you must do to deserve heaven and killing infidels is probably first on the list, but eternity is not about what we must do to deserve it.

What could we do to truly deserve God's attention, His love, if you will? Eternity in heaven is about what God has done for us in sending His son, His Son, not just a prophet, but the Son of God, Jesus Christ to pay a debt we could not pay so that we could live with Him forever in eternity."

Azziz grunted, turned over, wrapped himself in his cover and was silent. I went back to my own bed still shaking a little from the encounter with the cobra hoping I could sleep.

By now Azziz could ride and although he was careful of his wound he could sit a horse all day. He rode beside me on my spare mount. As we rode he would tell of the history of his people, the stories of the places he had seen. He had ridden and fought over much of the east from Egypt to Turkey as Saracen potentates fought among themselves for power and control. "

"But the knife, Sir Isaac, how did you come by the knife?" Malin's father asked before Sir Isaac could go down another trail. "By now it was December and the weather had turned cold and wet. He came to me just before we reached Jaffa.

I knew he would have to leave us or face death at the hands of Richard's army. Quietly he told me that over the time he was with us he had come to believe in Jesus Christ. "Where will you go?" I asked. "You can no longer live among your people." 'There are some among us who believe as you believe, Christian.

I will seek them out. I know you will not take my life in service for what you have done for me, but please accept this as a remembrance of me as a surety for the debt I owe. You I will keep in my heart.' And he gave me this dagger. That is the story." "And did you see him again?" Malin's father asked.

"No. We went to Jaffa and fought in the mud against the Saracens with King Richard until the peace was made. I traveled as I could to see where Jesus had walked. There were monasteries and churches that marked His steps that had been there for hundreds of years even then. The armies returned to their lands. Richard was taken captive and held ransom which had nothing to do with me and he was finally felled by a crossbow bolt after his ransom. I had long since lost all desire for battle. It was time after many years to return home. And here I am traveling still everywhere, not belonging anywhere; sharing your wonderful manor and King John is on the throne."

The tale over, the dinner broke up and the local guests went to their homes; those staying with Godric, Malin's father, to their beds. But the dagger burned its way into Malin's head.

He had never seen such a beautiful thing. He had held it in his hands. He had seen the workmanship. He had felt the weight of it. He had looked at the lines of the panther's body and wrapped his hand around the grip. He could feel it still in his hand. He saw the jewels glowing in the firelight in his mind's eye; each stone brilliant and perfect.

He wanted that dagger as he had never wanted anything in his young life. It filled his mind. It possessed him. He could not sleep for desire of it. He spent the night in fitful dreams of the dagger.

Malin's father, Godric, Sir Isaac and several others were leaving to hunt in the early morning through the woods and fields of his father's lands. Malin was still awake when his father came to rouse him. His father thought it was the excitement of the hunt that woke him early.

He was not aware of the turmoil in his son's heart. Malin went out with the others and stayed close to Sir Isaac as they rode. His father thought it was hero worship that drew him close to the older knight. It was the lure of the dagger.

Some were hunting with bow. Others had their falcons on their arms for pheasant and rabbits. A few hearty souls carried boar spears hoping the beaters would drive one of the ferocious beasts toward them. Malin had his bow, but it was not strung. He told his father he would be squire for Sir Isaac should it be required. He wanted to be close to the dagger.

Once they were deep into the woods there was little talk. They rode on toward a large meadow in the midst of the forest. The plan was to make camp on the edge of it and hunt on foot from there. The falconers would work the clearing. The others would stalk the woods. It was all good serious fun as his father would say.

The hunt went on throughout the day. Those hunting with falcons had done well early on taking a number of pheasant. They would try again later for rabbit when the meadow settled down again after their arrival. Sir Isaac picketed his horse with the others and set off on his own with Malin trailing close behind him keeping as quiet as he could. They had gone some distance when Sir Isaac put down a doe with one arrow. They eased up to the doe.

Sir Isaac made certain she was dead before he started to dress the carcass. He reached for his beautiful dagger and before Malin could stop himself he gasped loudly. Sir Isaac stopped and looked at him. Malin stared at the beautiful dagger in Isaac's hand. Sir Isaac saw the direction of his gaze and smiled, "Perhaps you are right. This dagger will not improve with deer blood covering it."

He put it back in its sheath and with that he pulled a smaller knife with a thinner blade from his boot top. They hauled the deer up with rope brought for the purpose and Sir Isaac dressed out the animal. "We should bear it back to camp."

So saying, Sir Isaac cut a long straight pole from a sapling fir, stripped it of needles and branches tied the legs of the doe together and they trudged back to camp carrying the doe between them.

As they neared the edge of the meadow where the camp was set the leather ties fastening the dagger to Sir Isaac's belt came loose and the dagger fell into the deep bracken of the woods.

Malin saw it fall and was about to say something when he suddenly closed his lips and in an instant kicked leaves to cover the dagger and walked on in one uninterrupted stride. He kept on walking but the phrase from the first Psalm came to him in his father's voice, "Blessed is the man who walks not in the counsel of the wicked." The plan had formed in his mind in an instant. He would come back later for the dagger and then it would be his.

The men were gathered about the camp talking and laughing. There was food and drink. Everyone was merry. There was the usual talk about the country under King John and if the French would attack soon and where would they land. There were reminiscences of hunts successful and otherwise.

Hunting stories were shared. Some might even have been true. The boar hunters returned with a kill so small the others wondered at it being allowed away from its mother. Some wit shouted, "It will be easy to clean, there are no bristles. It's not old enough to shave." Everyone laughed except the boar hunters. "Maybe you should have thrown it back until it grows bigger." Someone else called.

"So say you now, but wait 'til it's on your plate and tease me about it, friend." A boar hunter retorted. With the mention of food appetites were renewed and the party began to eat again. The day sped on as the hunting continued. The falconers were successful toward the end of the day and it was a joyful party that returned to the manor that night as darkness fell with meat aplenty and new stories to tell.

They were again gathered for a late supper when Sir Isaac realized his dagger was gone. There was an immediate search of his rooms and the household, but the beautiful dagger was nowhere to be found. "I must have lost it in the wood this morning. I remember drawing it to dress the deer and returning it to its sheath when young Malin objected to such a use as cleaning a deer. After that I do not know." "I will send my woodsman to search for it." Said Malin's father.

"I will go, Father." Malin volunteered. "I was with Sir Isaac this morning. I know where we were in the forest." "Sir Isaac, what would you desire?" Questioned Godric. "I have had the dagger a long time and its memory is precious to me.

I would be loathed to lose it, but if it is not found it is only a thing and the memory I carry with me always. Certainly, allow young Malin to search if he is in need of a quest." "So be it. Malin, leave at first light and return before dark."

It was all working according to Malin's plan. He would locate the dagger, hide it about him and return saying he could not find it. No one would question it. The wood was so large and the dagger so small. Then it would be his. Again he could see its jeweled beauty in his mind's eye. He would possess it. The meal finished and Malin spent another sleepless night waiting for the dawn.

 He set out early after breaking his fast with his father and Sir Isaac. There were many admonitions and directions about how careful he should be and what to do if there was a problem. Malin heard none of them. He escaped along the path through the woods confident he could find the dagger and possess it. As he walked the words of the Psalm came to him again in his father's voice, "Blessed is the man who walks not in the counsel of the wicked."

He knew with every step he took he was indeed walking in the counsel of the wicked, but still on he strode. This time he was not on horseback and the trip to the meadow took much longer than he remembered. He saw the larch tree on the edge of the meadow that marked his entrance into the forest with Sir Isaac. He knew they had headed east from there into the sun. Everything was the same this morning as he began to work his way through the wood. His eyes were set toward the ground and the small pile of bracken he had kicked over the dagger. As if drawn by an invisible thread he walked to a pile of leaves and began to brush then gently away. There was the dagger. It seemed to glow in the leafy darkness of the wood.

He retrieved the weapon and clutched it to his chest. His desire burned within him. He had the dagger. The want of it overwhelmed him and as he stood there with Sir Isaac's dagger held tightly to him the words of the Psalm came to him again. "Nor stands in the way of sinners," The very fact of his being here; standing here with this knife in his hands never intending to return it.

Intending to hide it; to keep it was testament to his wrong. He stood there for some moments and then the feeling came over him that he was being watched. Had someone followed him? Was Sir Isaac tracking him through the wood? Did he suspect what Malin had in mind? Malin turned swiftly dagger in hand to confront the danger. He was being watched. His heart went to his throat. Not Sir Isaac, but wolves. Wolves drawn by the carrion left from Sir Isaac's deer. They had come for the offal and now smelled fresh prey. Malin turned and began to run. He held the dagger tight in his grasp.

There was no thought of defending himself. When he ran the wolves began to pursue. Malin dodged in and out of the trees. He was running for his life.

He stumbled through the bracken turning first one way and then another; blindly running through the dense forest. His heart was pounding in his chest. He was gasping for breath. Ahead he spied a tree with low hanging branches and he raced toward it with the wolves snapping at his heels. Malin reached it and began to climb just as the lead wolf growled and lunged for him.

The wolf bit into Malin's shoe, but that was all he got. Malin climbed and climbed leaving the wolves howling, tearing at his shoe and barking behind him on the ground. He was out of their reach. He made his way to a heavy branch ten feet above the ground and sat down clutching the trunk of the tree; his chest heaving. He yelled at the wolves gathering below him to scare them off, but they howled all the more. And then the words of the Psalm returned to him again, "Nor sit in the seat of the scoffers." He had completed the decent. He had walked. He had stood and now he was sitting in the seat of the scoffers.

His desire for something that was not his had led him here and now he was trapped and with one look around he knew he was lost in the depth of the wood with no idea how to find his way home. He did not know how far he had run or in what direction. Clouds rolled in overhead he could no longer see the sun. He did not know east from west and the wolves circled and howled deprived of their prey.

The day turned to night and still the wolves paced and howled, tearing his leather shoe to small pieces.

Malin had been in the tree without food or water for many hours. With the coming of the night the deer began to move and the pack of wolves went off in search of other food that was easier to reach. Malin feared to get down lest the wolves return. He nestled closer to the tree and settled in for the rest of a miserable night. When the sun set he began to shiver with the cold. Over and over the verses in Psalms his father had taught him filled his mind, "Walketh not in the counsel of the wicked, nor stands in the way of sinners, nor sitteth in the seat of the scornful." And with each repetition he held tighter to the dagger.

He would not let it go even though he knew it was his desire that brought him to this place.

The fog and cold continued with the dawn. A hazy gray light filtered through the forest canopy. Malin still did not know east from west but as the light grew he could at least see enough of the ground to let himself softly down. The wolves were gone.

He was hungry, weary and frightened. He looked for something to eat, berries, even grass, but there was nothing. And he had only one shoe. His stomach growled with hunger. And then he smelled it. Food.

Someone was cooking nearby. If only he might see the smell then he could follow it, but still he let his nose lead him through the dense wood. He knew it couldn't be too far away or he would not smell the aroma of cooking. He made his way as silently as he could with one shoe missing.

There were some boulders ahead. He began to edge his way slowly around them. The smell was getting stronger. He drew the dagger thinking to surprise and threaten whoever it might be into giving him food. He began to quietly slip around the rocks. He was on the edge of the boulders now and could see a campsite with smoke coming from a fire and pot set over the flames. There was a magnificent horse hobbled with a pack mule beyond the blaze.

He was looking for its owner when there came a flash from nowhere and before he knew it the dagger had been struck from his hand and the flat of a sword struck him on the side of his head knocking him down.

Over him stood a dark skinned man clad in sumptuous robes. He held a long curved sword pointing at Malin's throat.

"Who are you?" Malin shouted angrily. "Who are you to be sneaking up on an innocent traveler with a dagger drawn in your hand?" Spoke the stranger. "Perhaps you are a common thief and I should take off your hand as I would were we in my country." Malin turned white as the blood rushed from his face. "Yes, a thief first loses a hand, then an arm and finally he is killed. But perhaps you are not a common thief. You must be a nobleman's son. No one else could be so arrogant and your clothes are nice if a bit dirty and worn."

"My name is Malin. I. . . I am lost in the woods. I got separated from our hunting party and spent the night in a tree. I smelled your fire and your food and found you. Perhaps you are the thief! You are a Saracen.

You are the enemy!" "If truly we were enemies you would be dead, young one, but I think you are lying. You have stolen this dagger. You have the look of the thief in your eye."

"The dagger is mine!" "I think not!" The Saracen raised his curved scimitar as if to strike. "Stop! Stop! Yes, yes, yes the dagger is stolen. I stole it."

Malin began to weep great heaving sobs. His fear, his sin, his hunger and his fatigue all caught up with him. "Here, take it." Malin sobbed as he pushed the dagger away from him. "Take it. Take it and let me go, please." The Saracen held out his hand to the boy. "Come, sit by the fire and eat. Then you can tell me your story." Malin hobbled over to the fire. With a slight limp the Saracen placed a small stone near the fire so that Malin would not have to sit on the ground. There was a pot with stew in it. The Saracen took some thick flat bread and scooped the stew onto it, cupped it and handed it to the boy. "Eat and then talk. I have water in a skin if you are thirsty."

Malin ate hungrily his sobs dying away as he ate. His eyes were still red and wet with tears. As he ate the Saracen looked at the dagger. A curious look came over his face.

After a time Malin began to speak. "You were right. The dagger is stolen. I saw it and wanted it. It is beautiful. Yesterday the owner dropped it in the woods while hunting and I saw where it had fallen. I covered it over with leaves and went silently home waiting for my chance.

If he did not notice I would go back later and get it. If he did I would volunteer to try to find it and come back without the dagger and that's what I did, but here were wolves. They chased me and I lost my bearings.

I did spend the night in a tree and I did smell your food. I wish I had never seen the dagger. I wish I had never taken it. Will they really cut my hand off?" "In my country? Yes, your hand would be cut off to remind you and others never to steal. But here in your country I think the law is more about restoration than retribution. Where is your village? I will see you home. You cannot walk with one shoe missing. This is the King's road we are on?" "Yes, yes, it goes right through our village."

When they had finished, the fire was put out and everything was packed on the mule and the Saracen mounted the great white stallion and then held out his hand to swing Malin up behind him.

The horse began at a slow walking pace making light of the new rider's weight. As they rode Malin told the story of the dagger to the Saracen. "I don't know what I will say to Sir Isaac. I feel so awful."

"Perhaps he will forgive you?" "He might, but my father won't. Sir Isaac is our guest. One doesn't steal from guests." "Or anyone else, young one. It is wrong." The stranger said.

Malin was silent for a moment and then he said, "I have never met a Saracen before. How did you come to our country?" "I have traveled long, young one. Many months it has taken me to travel from the east to your island." But as the Saracen spoke he realized he was talking to himself. Malin had fallen asleep upright at his back. The Saracen smiled and rode on in silence. After a time they came to a village. There were people working fields and a priory on the edge of the village. The Saracen reached back and shook Malin gently by the leg. "Boy, boy, is this your village?"

With a start Malin was awake looking around him. He saw the priory with the monks going in and out. Their long robes gathered up as they worked in the fields. "Our manor is on the far side of the village set back from the road." They went on collecting strange looks from the people they met. "I think you are not the only one who's never seen a Saracen, boy. I hope we make it to your father's manor."

As they drew closer Malin's fear grew. He did not want to face his father or Sir Isaac.

There was a large crowd in his father's yard; men and horses. "What is going on?" Malin said. "Can you not guess? They are about to search for a boy lost in the woods. They are about to go hunting for you." As they rode in to the manor gates the crowd turned slowly toward them.

The older men put their hands to their swords. One archer drew back his bow. The Saracen stopped. His stallion tossed his head up and down in the silence.

A voice rang out, "What do you here, Saracen?" "I think I have discovered what you seek. The lost has been found." And with that he swung Malin to the ground and dismounted himself.

"Malin? Malin, we were just going out to search for you." Godric said as he threw his arms around his son. "You may not wish to embrace me Father. I went out to get the dagger Sir Isaac had dropped. I saw it fall. I covered it up. I was going to steal it. To keep it. I'm sorry. Please forgive me. This man found me in the wood. He fed me and brought me here."

"It is not my forgiveness you need, but Sir Isaac's. It is he you have wronged." During this encounter Sir Isaac had made his way to the front of the crowd near Godric and Malin. "Sir Isaac, please forgive me. I wanted your dagger and so I took it. It was wrong. Please forgive me." "You are forgiven, my boy, but it is not my dagger. You have returned it to its rightful owner. This Saracen is Azziz of whom I spoke. It should be restored to him. He has returned a life for a life, your life for his life the surety has been met, the debt is paid. Sir Isaac rushed to his old friend and embraced him. "I thought never to see you again, my friend." "The wars continued and there was no place for me in my homeland any longer. I made my way here to find you and find you I have by the grace of God and Jesus Christ our Savior.

And grace is what I hope will be granted to this young one. He has been chased by wolves. He has spent the night by himself in the forest. He has gone hungry. He has seen the destruction that desire and greed can cause. He has seen that the way of the transgressor is hard. "

The End.

ABOUT THE AUTHOR

Mr. Whitley grew up in eastern North Carolina. At the age of four he came in childlike faith to Jesus Christ. He dedicated his life to Christ while on a church camp-out at the age of eleven. Doug has worked as a sponsor to both Junior and Senior High young people. He has coached state championship soccer teams and conference championship teams on the college level and took one team to the finals on the national level.

Mr. Whitley holds a B.A. in speech and an M.A. in dramatic production.

Doug began his present ministry in August of 1990 after breaking his arms while wiring a friend's barn. Doug and his wife, Cheri travel together trusting the Lord to meet their needs. The ministry has taken them from coast to coast, North to South and literally around the world presenting God's Truth through the lives of these heroes of the faith. In portraying the lives of these men, Doug feels not only their burden for others, but the burden of portraying men who were giants of the faith.

CONTACT: www.preachersofthepast.com

Made in the USA
Middletown, DE
30 March 2023

27908039R00125